COMMUNITY COLLEGES IN INDIA

COMMUNITY COLLEGES IN INDIA

Education For Livelihood

Dr. Xavier Alphonse, S.J.

GYAN PUBLISHING HOUSE
New Delhi - 110002

Community Colleges in India: Education for Livelihood

ISBN : 81-212-0904-8

Rs. 650

Published in 2007 in India by
Gyan Publishing House
5, Ansari Road, Daryaganj,
New Delhi - 110002
e-mail : books@gyanbooks.com
website : gyanbooks.com

Laser Typesetting at : Vinayak Printers, Delhi
Printed at : Salasar Imaging System, Delhi

Contents

Introduction

I am very happy to present this book and dedicate the same to the millions of young men and women in India who are looking for a break in their lives with hope and enthusiasm.

The journey towards the Community College System has been a personal journey and an answer to the personal search of my own on the questions of flexibility, opportunity, access and cost effectiveness in our Higher Education. The Jesuit order gave me an opportunity to be the Principal of Loyola College (Autonomous), Chennai one of the premier institutions in the country during the year 1992-1995. The most difficult time for a principal of such a college is the admission time when crowds of people throng to the campus to seek an opportunity for Higher Education in the institution. I used to get 18,000 applications for 1000 seats. Hundreds of people used to wait to meet the principal. I used to be flooded with the recommendations from the high and the mighty, the influential and the powerful.

In this whole process the people who are left out are the marginalised and the rural poor who are unable to get into such institutions. The whole question of Higher Education lies on the basis of access and equity. This question set me thinking where will all these thousands of people go when they are denied admissions into under graduate courses. They have no alternative system of education in which they can easily find the means to improve their livelihood.

It is at this point of time, I was introduced to the *Community College System in USA*. I visited 18 Community Colleges during 1995–1996. I was amazed at the flexibility and the Opportunity given to the weaker sections in the Colleges. The Community

Colleges are known in USA as Democratic Colleges / People's Colleges. I could see thousands of people benefiting by the system. There is no age bar, no minimum qualification. There is total flexibility in the teaching and evaluation and a wonderful chance to improve one's skills to become employable. 52% of the population go to 1100 Community Colleges and they pay the minimum cost of 1200 dollars per year. The Community Colleges offer 2 year associate degree with the possibility of vertical mobility through credit transfer to the graduate course in the country. The whole process inspired me and made me ask questions in the context of India.

Can we workout a similar system in India?

Who could be the target group of the system?

Which are the agencies that could implement the system.

The answers to the above questions gave birth to the local indigenous Indian Community College System *that is described in detail in this book.*

In August 1996 we started the first Community College by an NGO the Arch-diocese of Madras-Mylapore *Madras Community College.* We offered them Life Skills, Work Skills, Internship leading to job placement. The idea spread to various NGOs in Tamilnadu and by the year 2000, *52 Community Colleges* started in Tamilnadu.

In the year 1999, we started the *Madras Centre for Research and Development of Community Education (MCRDCE)* a co-ordinating and facilitating agency for all Community Colleges in India with a clear motto of *Including the Excluded and Giving the best to the Least.* Today the movement has spread far and wide, and today we have 154 Community Colleges in 17 States of India.

1	Tamil Nadu	98	2	Pondicherry	03
3	Andhra Pradesh	07	4	Delhi	01
5	Karnataka	11	6	Kerala	09
7	Maharashtra	02	8	Madhya Pardesh	04
9	Gujarat	02	10	Jharkhand	07
11	Uttaranchal	01	12	Chhattisgarh	03
13	Goa	01	14	Orissa	01
15	Himachal Pradesh	01	16	Uttar Pradesh	01
17	West Bengal	01		Total	154

The Book is written to give a clear articulation and formulation to the Indian Community College System in all its aspects.

Part I – Introduction

Chapter 1	The Concept of Community College
Chapter 2	The Seven Stages of Preparation
Chapter 3	Need Analysis
Chapter 4	Curriculum Development
Chapter 5	Life Skills
Chapter 6	Work Skills
Chapter 7	Evaluation and Assessment of Skills
Chapter 8	Internship and Hands on Experience
Chapter 9	Preparation for Employment
Chapter 10	Industrial Community Partnership
Chapter 11	Self Employment
Chapter 12	Administration and Governance of Community Colleges
Chapter 13	Recognition and Accreditation of Community Colleges

Part II – The Contribution of MCRDCE

Chapter 14	The Contribution of MCRDCE to the Community College Movement
Chapter 15	Profile of the Rural Community College
Chapter 16	The Role of the Universities
Chapter 17	Directory of Community Colleges and the Courses given
Chapter 18	Target Group Served
Chapter 19	Indian Community College System
Chapter 20	Publications
Chapter 21	Conclusion
Chapter 22	Bibliography

We have achieved a clear profile of the Urban Community Colleges. We have discovered the seeds of the profile of Rural Community College. We have designed the curriculum for employability. We have created 25,000 Miracles of Hope. I thank all the Administrators, Faculty Members, Students, Parents, Industrial and Community Partnership and all the Community Colleges in India without whose collaboration and experience the writing of this book is not possible.

I thank the MCRDCE team, Mr. Joseph Johnson, Mr. Jothilingam, Mr. Senthilkumar, Ms. Greta Suganya, Ms. Alphonsia Rani, Ms. Maria Jothi for their whole hearted cooperation in the production of the book and the documentation of the entire process from 1993.

I thank the Gyan Publishing House who have come forward to bring out this as part of their educational service in introducing this innovative concept to the whole country.

I wish that the reading of this book will lead and guide the service minded NGOs to implement this alternative system of education in favour of the marginalised which will build a strong and vibrant India.

Dr. Xavier Alphonse, S.J.,
Director, MCRDCE, Chennai
26.01.2006

1
The Concept of Community College

1.1 Introduction

During the last ten years the Concept of Community College has gained clarity and focus. The concept that is articulated below is the fruit of the experimentation and experience of many Community Colleges, National and Regional Seminars and Consultations conducted on *Community College as an Alternative System of Education in India.*

The Concept of the Community College may have taken its roots on the American Soil and would have given us an inspiration to follow a similar system in India. What is articulated below is nothing to do with the US reality. The concept has gone through a complete transformation to suit and respond to the Indian Reality. It is thoroughly *Local* and *Indigenous.*

1.2 The Concept of Community College

- The Community College is an alternative system of education, which is aimed at the empowerment of the disadvantaged and the underprivileged. (Urban poor, rural poor, tribal poor and women) through appropriate skills development leading to gainful employment in collaboration with the local industry and the community and achieve skills for employment and self employability of the above sections of people in the society.
- The Community College is an innovative educational alternative that is rooted in the community providing

holistic education and eligibility for employment to the disadvantaged.

- The Vision of the Community College is to be of the Community, for the Community and by the Community and to produce responsible citizens.
- The Community College promotes *job oriented, work related, skill - based and life coping education.*
- The Community College initiative is in conformity with the Indian political will that prioritises in education, primary education, information technology education and vocational education.
- The key words of the Community College system are *access, flexibility in curriculum and teaching methodology, cost effectiveness and equal opportunity in collaboration with industrial, commercial and service sectors of the local area and responding to the social needs and issues of the local community, internship and job placement within the local area, promotion of self employment and small business development, declaration of competence and eligibility for employment.*

1.3 The Community College – Need of the Hour

- The Community College is the significant need of the hour in the context of the problems of *Unemployment, Under Employment* and *Unemployability*. The need for the Community College system has emerged on account of the high percentage of *Exclusion and Elimination* from the formal system of education. In India there are 90 Million in the age group of 14 to 18 years. At present, 20 Million are in schools and colleges and 70 Million are out of the formal educational system. 160 million children go to the first standard, only 6 Million children reach the college level. The above numbers clearly show there are more young men and women out of School and College. There is also the problem of *Mismatch between Education and Employment*, which is seen in the number of educated applicants registered at the Employment Exchanges all over the country.

- There are 42 Lakhs of registered educated unemployed in Tamil Nadu. The overall scenario in India is very distressing.

- *"Unemployment* is the root cause of multifarious problems prevalent in our country today", said *Former Defence Minister George Fernandes.* The political extremism being faced by several states of India today owed its origin to the state of unemployment in the country. The number of *Educated Unemployed* in 1995 was 3.65 crore. It had increased to 4.14 crore in 2000. This showed an increase of 10 Lakh unemployed every year. Employment opportunities with this ratio were difficult to generate. *(Hindustan Times, New Delhi, March 6, 2001).*

- *Exclusion and Elimination* -154 Million out of the 160 Million who go to the first standard in India.

- *Mismatch between Education and Employment* 4 Crores and 15 Lakhs (India) 42 Lakhs (Tamil Nadu)

- *Capability Poverty* – There is the lack of capability and competencies in 554 Million people in India. *(UNDP Report 1996).*

- Human Development Index India ranks 115 in the world *(UNDP Report 2001).*

- According to the *ILO Report June 2001*, 160 Million are openly unemployed in the World. One Billion if underemployed are also included. For every 100 workers 6 are fully unemployed and 16 are unable to earn 1$ per person per day. *(The Hindu, June 28, 2001).*

- Though *63.04 lakhs* students get admitted in *31,052 schools* across the state, the drop-out rate is almost *36 per cent* by the time they get to high school of which *90 per cent* are girls. *(The New Indian Express, January 9, 2002).*

- Around *48 Lakh "Non-School Going" Children* (in the 6 - 14 age group) in Tamil Nadu. *(The New Indian Express, January 9, 2002).*

- During the month of September in 2002, 939 employment exchanges all over the country had registered 4 crore and 16 lakh of which 70% are educated. *(Dinamani, 28.02.2003)*

- The School Droupouts in Tamil Nadu

Primary Stage	- 1998 - 1999	- 14.52%
	- 1999 - 2000	- 14.41%
	- 2000 - 2001	- 14.40%
Middle Stage	- 1998 - 1999	- 35.23%
	- 1999 - 2000	- 35.43%
	- 2000 - 2001	- 35.59%
High School Stage	- 1998 - 1999	- 81%
	- 1999 - 2000	- 57.9%
	- 2000 - 2001	- 89%
Higher Secondary Stage	- 1998 - 1999	- 81%
	- 1999 - 2000	- 89.27%
	- 2000 - 2001	- 82.30%

❑ The above Information collected from National Information Centre, Vellore - *December 2001.*

❑ *The above picture clearly indicates the High Percentage of dropouts at the High School and Higher Secondary School Stages which call for An Alternative System of Education like the Community Colleges.*

- We find that if 100 million students get enrolled in the primary school, only about 30 million are found in middle school and about 16 million in high/higher secondary school. Of children in the age group 6-11 years. About 90-95 percent enrol in primary school, at the secondary stage, that is, age group 11-15 years, only 48 percent continue and at the higher secondary stage, that is, age group 15-17 years, only about 24 per cent are found to pursue studies. In the age group 17 to 23, only about eight percent are in the higher educational institutions.

- From these statistics, we can see that roughly, above 50 per cent of students drop out at every stage, in the school. The questions that arise are, what happens to all those youth who drop out of the educational system between the age group 11-17 years? *(The Hindu, Open Page, Tuesday, July 23, 2002)*

- **Mr. Chidambaram** said over 50 percent of the children in the country were school dropouts before they completed five years of education.
- A million children, especially in Rajasthan, Bihar, Uttar Pradesh, Madhya Pradesh and Orissa, did not complete three or four years of schooling every year, he said.
- Dubbing it a *"colossal waste of human resources"*, he said it was a shame that the country, even after 57 years of Independence, was not able to make elementary education universal and compulsory. *(The Hindu, Chennai, 04.08.2004, p.11)*
- **World Watch Organisation gives the following details.**
    - 10 million Children do not go to school in the world.
    - In many countries 75% stop with 5th Std.
    - One third of this 75% are girls.
    - In illiteracy India stands 127th among the 177 countries of the world. *(Dinamalar, 22.05.2005, p.15)*

1.4 The Salient features of the Community College System:

- The Community Colleges should be established by a *Non-Profit Making, Non-Commercial* and *Community Based Organisation* with proven years of service to the local community.
- The establishment of the Community Colleges should by preceded by an extensive *Need Analysis* of the employment opportunities available in the local area and also *the Social Needs* of the Community.
- The *Target Group* of the Community College is 12th passed students, 10th passed students, school drop outs, rural youth, rural women, existing workforce that wants to update its skills and all who want skill based and need based education at an affordable price.

- There is *No Age Limit* for admission into a Community College.
- The close and active linkage between *Industries and Community Colleges* is a must for the success of the Community College System *The Industrial Partners* help the College in designing the curriculum, providing part time instructors, serving as members of the advisory board and the governing board, taking students for internship and helping them to find job placement.
- The Community College is a *Multi-Campus Reality.*
- The Community College is permitted to the optimum utilisation of the *existing infrastructural facilities* available to the community-based organisation that establishes the Community College and also to reduce the cost of the training.
- The Community College tries to respond to the deficiencies of the Vocational System through Industry–Institutional Linkage, competence assessment, proper certification, training on site, life skills training and job oriented programmes decided on the basis of the local needs.
- It is in the above areas that the Community College is an improvement and departure from earlier initiatives such as ITIs, Community Polytechnics and apprenticeship training and plus two vocationalisation of education.
- The *Curriculum* of the Community College has four distinct parts: *Life Skills, Work Skills, Internship* and *Preparation for Employment.* The certificate programmes for the school dropouts consist of 28 weeks and the diploma programmes consist of 52 weeks for the 10th and 12th passed students and all others who want skill – based education.
- The *Evaluation and Assessment of Skills* done by the Community College has four dimensions: *Self-Assessment, Assessment by the Life Skills and Work Skills teachers and internship supervisor at the work spot.*

- The course fees charged from the recipients of the Community College System should be cost effective and affordable as per the document submitted to the Government of Tamil Nadu. *Computer – Rs.5,000, Technical – Rs.4,500 and Non Technical – Rs.4,000.*
- The creation of The Community College is in accordance with the Programme of action of *NPE–1992* that recommends the establishment of Community Colleges in India : *"To encourage establishment of Community Colleges dealing with vocationalisation of subjects related to service sector on line with Community polytechnics".*

1.5 The Differences between the Community College System and other Formal Systems of Vocational Education:

There are various formal systems of Vocational Education in Operation in India such as;

(a) Apprenticeship Training

(b) Plus Two Vocational system in schools

(c) Industrial Technical Institutes (ITI)

(d) Community Polytechnics.

(e) Vocationalisation of first degree level Education at the Collegiate Level.

These systems have experienced certain deficiencies and difficulties. The Community College System as an Alternative and Innovative System tries to remedy the above deficiencies.

1. It is aiming at the employability of the individual trained.
2. It is evolving a system to declare the competency level and duly certify the same.
3. It is promoting strong Industry – Institutional linkage and ties. It involves the Industry to articulate the skills, it wants and works in close collaboration with industries to make the individuals skill oriented that is needed by the employer.

4. It emphasises the teaching of the Life Skills, Communication Skills and English to the takers of the system.
5. The Community College system certainly lessens the burden on higher Education.
6. It is evolving a system of evaluation and assessment of skills, which are personal. Social, language, communication, work and creative.

2

The Seven Stages of Preparation

2.1 Introduction

The establishment of a Community College is a careful process of Planning and Implementation. The MCRDCE has guided *154 Community College*s and it is helping 40 more towards the proper establishment of these institutions all over the country. The stages given below have been gone through by the above institutions. *Mr. Anto Vincent,* has shared these stages to most of the groups who have taken part in the workshops organised by MCRDCE all over India.

2.2 The Seven Stages of preparation towards the Establishment of a Community College

Planning: "If I have eight hours to chop a tree, I will spend six sharpening the axe" - *Abraham Lincoln*

Stage - I
Understanding the Concept

- A People's Movement
- Changing Track
- Including the Excluded
- Aligning Education with Employment
- Best to the Least (capability poor)
- Job Oriented-Work Related-Skill Based and Life Coping Education
- Accessibility (to Students, Community and Industry)

- Flexibility (in Curriculum and Teaching Methodology)
- Cost Effective
- Equal Opportunity
- Collaboration (with Industry, Society and Community)
- Non Profit making, Non Commercial

Stage - II
Need Analysis

- Employment Opportunities available
- Availability in the Local Area
- Responding to the Needs of the Local Community
- Social Needs of the Society
- Based on Emerging Economic / Industrial Pattern
- Trend in Population Growth
- Preserving Local Talent / Skill / Unique Capabilities
- Proximity to Community: Proximity to Industry

Stage -III
Main Anchor of Community College Movement

Active Participati on and Collaboration of:

- Industry
- Rural
- Agricultural
- Commercial and
- Service Organisations

Industrial Partnership helps Community Colleges in the following ways:

1. Designing the Curriculum for Job Oriented Courses
2. Serving as members of the Advisory Board ....
3. Part Time Instructors for Teaching and .....
4. On the job training for students in the work place ...
5. Job Placement for students who have been trained...

How to go about?

1. List out neighbourhood industries .....
2. Conduct a need analysis study ...
3. Contact the industrial chiefs and explain mission...
4. Form IP Core group and meet periodically
5. Invite prominent leaders to be a Board Members
6. Form a Task Force to work out the syllabus
7. Keep IPC Group members updated on progress
8. Enlist volunteers from industry to be faculty
9. Include IPC Group members in admission

Industrial Partnership some Tips:

- Desirability of signing a MOU
- Keep continuous contact (Eg: Madurai Community College)
- Not excluding Industrial Partners
- Give them credit for accomplishments
- Involve industry right from beginning and at each step
- Offer to train employees of industries in life skills, specific technical skills etc., (Eg: Madurai)
- Offer as an outsource agency

Stage - IV
Deciding the Job Oriented Programmes to be Given

- Choose the right course
- Course that meets every need- need of the industry* need of the Community* need of the students.
- Health
- Rural Development
- Agriculture
- Technical
- Non-Technical
- Self employment and Small Business Development

In Collaboration with the practitioners of the Industry, Commerce, Service, Agricultural and Rural Sector

- Based on funding, infrastructure
- Based on future requirements
- Based on the aspiration of the youth
- Based on Availability of the teaching staff

Course Contents

- Life Skills
- Work Skills
- Internship
- Preparation for employment
- Possibilities of entrepreneurship
- Certificate programme for 28 weeks
- Diploma programme for 52 weeks

Some Thoughts:

- Start with the least expensive
- Start one or two courses
- Additional courses at staggered intervals
- Periodically revise the syllabus to cope with the changes in the market place

Stage -V
Feasibility Study

- Capability to mobilize funds
- Capability of the students to pay: Alternately, Capability to subsidize course fee
- Availability of infrastructure: building, class rooms, furniture etc.
- Capability to pay rent in the absence of building
- Possibility of industrial partnership

- Location of place-conducive to learn
- Availability of the teaching staff

Questions to ask ourselves:

- AM I BEING PRACTICAL?
- IS MY PROPOSAL COST EFFECTIVE?
- WILL I BE IN A POSITION TO SUSTAIN THROUGH FOR 12 MONTHS?
- THERE COULD BE HURDLES ON THE WAY, DO I HAVE THE WILL TO PERSEVERE?
- AM I CLEAR ABOUT THE MISSION?

Stage - VI
Recruitment of Teachers

- Competent Teachers
- Committed to the Mission
- Service as the Prime Motive
- Balanced in Life
- Having the right attitude/Aptitude
- Possible role models
- Willingness to learn new skills

Some thoughts:

- Associate IPs in the selection process ...
- Start with minimum number of teachers
- Develop them in decision making
- Involve them in decision making
- Update the skills of teachers
- Continuous motivation

Stage - VII
Admission of Students

Target Group:

- 12th Standard passed
- 10th Standard Passed
- School Drop-outs
- Rural Youth
- Rural Women
- Existing workforce
- No Age Limit
- Underprivileged
- Suggested Minimum 25

Some Thoughts?????

- Collection of fee? - Value of anything given free?
- Suggested Rs. 5,000 (Computer): Rs. 4,500 (Tech) and Rs. 4,000 (Non-Tech)
- Pro-active exemption/reduction for truly deserving
- Solid base for funding essential before you venture
- Also for self employment/Small business
- Evaluation system and methodology
- Life skill mandatory
- 3 Hours and 6 Hours

Fit for Life to Run and To Win Confidently

What Should You Be?

- Passionate
- Committed
- Flexible
- Persevering
- Patient
- Loving
- Humble
- Goal Oriented

3
Need Analysis

3.1 Introduction

Need Analysis is the back bone of the Community College. It is considered to be the Gospel of the Community College. The Community College is established on the firm footing and foundation of the thorough Need Analysis of the Employment and Self-Employment Opportunities in the Local Area. The MCRDCE has done and helped more than 100 institutions to do their Need Analysis. What is presented below is the fruit of the experience of the Need Analysis done so far.

3.2 The Concept, Philosophy and Methodology of Need Analysis

Philosophy

- Facts Vs Notion
- Feasibility Search
- Possibility Exploration (Looking beyond visible realities)
- Pulse of the Community (people's movement)
- Creating awareness
- Enlisting Collaboration from step one
- Path finding

Need Analysis Directions

- Nomenclature
- The Approach - Not "Excluded"
- Entrepreneurship

- Rural/Home Based
- Call of the Territory
- Existing People - Improve
- Positive Appeal
- Need to enrol people's Acceptance

Need Analysis Objectives

- Identify Opportunities and Possibilities
- Understand Job Descriptions and Skills Requirement (In rural methods and skills requirement)
- Identify Possible Programmes
- Assess overall feasibility

Need Analysis Data Collection

- *Primary Data*
- *Secondary Data*

Primary Data (Concerning the employer and job opportunities as perceived by the employer)

- Name and address
- Respondent - who is she / he
- Nature of business / activity
- Job availability by year 2004 (numbers)
- Jobs - nature (by name)
- Skills required
- Interest on collaboration (Curriculum, Internship, Faculty and Employment)

Secondary Data (Educational and employment scenario from indirect sources)

- Telephone Directory / Yellow pages
- Inspector of labour / factories
- Association Directories
- District Education Officer
- District Employment Officer

Survey Methods

- Questionnaire
- Personal Interview
- Data Collection from Administrative and other Sources
- Visits to field (Ground Realities)

Designing the Questionnaire

- Adequate
- Crisp
- Leave Out Trivials
- Non Embarrassing
- Visual Appeal of the Instrument
- Questions Leading to Statistical Applications
- Questions Leading to Statistical Applications (Number, Scale, List items, Responsive like "Yes / No / Do not know")
- Room for Respondent Contribution
- Flexibility in Questionnaire (Ask right questions - Different strokes for different folks.

Beyond The Need Analysis

- Finding empty cups
- Risk Taking
- Intuition
- Visionary
- Missionary
- Patience
- Perseverance
- Preparedness
- Possibilities
- Potentials (latent)

Impediments

- Non interest - Respondent Data Collector
- Time

- Energy
- Finance
- Ineffective Questionnaire
- Complacency
- Compromise
- Impatience
- Jumping into Conclusions
- Mental Blocks (Prove what I have in mind)

Who Conducts the Survey?

- Consultants
- Research Scholars
- Paid Survey Workers
- NGOs having expertise
- Task Force
- Animators

Useful Hints

- Total Commitment
- Plan itinerary for optimal Time Management and for minimizing travel
- Concept propaganda
- Be ready for questions (brain storm on possible questions. Let some one be Devil's advocate)
- Use existing reports
- Diplomatic approach
- Confidentiality

Possible Areas

- Technical
- Non Technical
- Agricultural
- Forestry

- Village Requirements
- Weaving
- Handloom
- Handicrafts
- Piggery
- Poultry
- Bee Keeping
- Herbal Farming
- Herbal Medicines
- Health
- Rain Water Harvest
- Data Entry Operator
- Hardware Mechanism
- Plumbing / Electrician
- Self Employment
- Kitchen Garden
- Food Products / Bakery

Call of the Territory

- Self esteem - Refusal to accept as disadvantaged
- Nomenclature
- Resistance to new concepts
- 100% Literacy
- Inadequacy of Higher Education
- Mobility - Inland and Overseas
- Lack of Industrial Growth
- Emotional attachment / opposition to ideas

3.3 Questionnaire used for the Need Analysis to collect the data from Potential Employers.

1. Name and Address of the Organisation.
2. Name of the Respondent and his/her Designation

3. Nature of the Business / Activity
4. No. of employees on the Rolls
5. How many jobs would be available by the year 2005
6. What are the new position (Jobs) that would be available? (By Name)

(a)________________ (d)________________

(b)________________ (e)________________

(c)________________ (f)________________

7. What are the skills required to perform the jobs available?

(a) Skill ______ (b) Skill ______ (c) Skill ______

______ ______ ______

______ ______ ______

______ ______ ______

(d) Skill ______ (e) Skill ______ (f) Skill ______

______ ______ ______

______ ______ ______

______ ______ ______

8. Would you be *interested* in collaborating in this Venture?

Yes/ No. If yes by what means?

(a) Designing the Curriculum (b) Teaching the students.

(c) Training the students (Internship) (d) Recruitment Students / Job Placement.

3.4 Samples of Need Analysis

Table I. Madurai Region Need Analysis at a Glance, April 1997

S.No	*Areas of Employment Potential*	*Units*	*No. of Jobs available*
1.	Textile Technology	35	1000
2.	Printing Technology	105	1500
3.	Hospitals and Allied Health services	86	1200
4.	Sales and Marketing Management	33	3000
5.	Automobile Service and Maintenance	67	4500
6.	Cargo Management	25	1250
7.	Small Business Management	500	Innumerable
8.	Soft Beverages Manufacturing	11	750
9.	Office Technology		2500

(Table I contd.)

10.	Small Home Appliances Service and Repair		1000
11.	Construction Management and Interior Decoration	22	500
12.	Computer Hardware and Software	52	Innumerable
13.	Air-Conditioning and Refrigeration		750
14.	Transport Fleet Management	67	1000
15.	Plantations Management	-	500
	Total		**19,450**

Table II. Chennai Region Need Analysis at a Glance, November 1997

S. No	*Areas of Employment Potential*	*Units*	*No. of Jobs available*
1.	Advertisement	78	2000
2.	Air Conditioning and Refrigeration	45	4000
3.	Aqua Culture	19	1000
4.	Automobile Service and Manufacturing	17	2600
5.	Bakery and Confectionery	24	1300
6.	Beautician and Health Care	27	570
7.	Book Publishing and Selling	120	5500
8.	Cargo Management	103	11800
9.	Commercial Photography	36	750
10.	Computer Hardware	100	1000
11.	Computer Software	348	78750
12.	Courier Services	108	18000
13.	Construction Management	98	16500
14.	Dairy Farming	13	850
15.	Export Garments Manufacturing	152	20000
16.	Fashion Designing	13	350
17.	Horticulture	12	850
18.	Hospitals and Allied Services	86	18000
19.	Hotel Management and Hospitality Services	120	19000
20.	Interior Decoration	163	12000
21.	Journalism	21	1500
22.	Office Management and Secretaryship	80	5000
23.	Plantation Management	14	400
24.	Printing Technology	224	8500
25.	Road Transport Management	207	12100
26.	Sales and Marketing Management	55	11000
27.	Small Home Appliances Repair and Service	135	8500
28.	Soft and Hard Manufacturing	16	1500
29.	Travel and Tourism Operations	254	14000
30.	Two Wheeler Mechanism	30	4200
31.	Visual and Graphics Mixing	22	350
32.	Courier Services	108	18000
	Total		**3,97,270**

Table III. Salem Region Need Analysis at a Glance, April 1998

S.No	*Areas of Employment Potential*	*Units*	*No. of Jobs available*
1.	Construction Management	50	640
2.	Automobile Maintenance and Service	50	1550
3.	Sago Manufacturing Supervisory	250	5625
4.	Hospital Management	70	1456
5.	Textile Technology	150	13200
6.	Two Wheeler Mechanism	25	1025
7.	Road Transport Management	150	2700
8.	Automobile Body Building	150	2020
9.	Community Health Worker and Service	25	155
10.	Computer Software	50	505
11.	Printing Technology	250	1525
12.	Sales and Marketing	35	315
13.	Mining Industry	75	900
14.	Granite Industry	50	1950
15.	Allied Industries with Salem Steel Plant	100	920
16.	Multi Skill Mechanic	50	5345
17.	Dairy Farming	35	136
18.	Small Home Appliances Service and Repair	75	900
19.	Poultry Management	150	1170
20.	Hotel Management	22	726
21.	Horticulture of Plantation Management	30	180
22.	Office Technology	45	436
	Total		**44,468**

Table IV. Nellai and Tuticorin Region Need Analysis at a glance, April 1998

S.No	*Areas of Employment Potential*	*Units*	*No. of Jobs availab le*
1.	Female Nursing Assistant	102	882
2.	Medical Lab Technician	104	634
3.	Radiographic and Scanning Assistant	28	98
4.	Theatre Assistant	102	505
5.	Pharmaceutical Assistant	49	220
6.	Community Development and Health Worker	246	3653
7.	Pre – School Teacher	121	950
8.	Multi Purpose Farm Supervisor	40	210
9.	Construction Management	170	1972
10.	Four Wheeler Mechanism	174	3010
11.	Two Wheeler Mechanism	129	1683
12.	Printing Technology	139	2690

(Table IV contd.)

13.	Computer Software Technology	97	1804
14.	Tiles Manufacturing Technology	34	1448
15.	Shipping (Cargo) Management	61	1312
16.	Sales and Marketing Management	81	1422
17.	Office Accountant and Secretaryship	103	1602
18.	Security Service	5	720
19.	Transport Fleet Management	19	351
20.	Home Appliances Service and Maintenance	33	377
21.	Wood Carving (Kadaisal)	45	594
	Total		**26,137**

Table V. Periyakulam Region Need Analysis at a Glance, October 1998

S.No	*Areas of Employment Potential*	*Units*	*No. of Jobs available*
1.	Nursing Assistants	124	1357
2.	Paramedical Assistants	215	860
3.	Textile Technology	81	5680
4.	Computer Software	43	555
5.	Ticketing and Tourism Development	63	536
6.	Hotel Management	30	825
7.	Horticulture and Plantation	34	1217
8.	Small Business Development	101	919
9.	Pre-School Teachers	40	444
10.	Dairy Farms	72	1448
11.	Tailoring, embroidering and dress making	40	620
12.	Home appliances maintenance and service	69	750
13.	Two wheelers mechanism	50	465
14.	Four wheelers mechanism	236	3975
15.	Beautician and skin care	20	70
	Total		**19,691**

Table VI. Tenali and Nallapadu Region Need Analysis at a Glance, June 1999

S.No	*Areas of Employment Potential*	*Units*	*No. of Jobs available*
1.	Computer Applications	192	1920
2.	Office Assistance (Chit funds)	311	1244
3.	Fast Food preparation (Bakery and Confectionery, Swagruha)	192	1088
4.	Screen Printing and Photo Lamination	78	780
5.	Medical Lab Assistance and Nursing Assistance	142	710
6.	Home Appliances (Servicing and Repair)	233	699
7.	Two-Wheeler Mechanism	25	500
8.	Small Scale Industrial Units (Soaps, Detergents, Brick Making, Vermiculture, etc.,)	38	380
9.	Photography	140	280
10.	Beauty Care and Health	65	195
11.	Hotel Receptionist	10	160
12.	Social Service Organisations for Rural Development	19	114
13.	Tailoring and Embroidery	18	54
	Total		**8,124**

Table VII. Devakottai Region Need Analysis at a glance, August 1999

S.No	*Areas of Employment Potential*	*Units*	*No. of Jobs available*
1.	Nursing Assistance	67	972
2.	Hospital Management	46	225
3.	Medical Lab Technician	35	91
4.	Pharmacy Assistance	98	412
5.	Computer Software Technology	28	176
6.	Pre-School Teachers	56	577
7.	Two Wheeler Mechanism	67	462
8.	Home Appliances Service and Maintenance	102	439
9.	Printing Technology	54	221
10.	Commercial Photography	53	228
	Total		**3,803**

Table VIII. Roorkee Need Analysis at a Glance, May 2000

S.No	*Areas of Employment*	*Total No. of Units in the area of Employment*	*Total No. of Jobs Up To 2005 AD*
1.	Nursing Assistant	179	2846
2.	Hospital Management	44	229
3.	Laboratory Technician	36	230
4.	Chemist Assistant	213	426
5.	X - Ray Technician	33	99
6.	O. T. Assistant	53	143
7.	Pharmaceutical Sales Management	92	3275
8.	Community Development Workers	103	2575
9.	Pre- school Teachers	74	1087
10.	Sugar Processing Technology	42	126
11.	Horticulture	44	726
12.	Computer Software	96	1258
13.	Computer Hardware	58	824
14.	Home Appliances Service and Maintenance	149	834
15.	Four Wheeler Mechanism	129	877
16.	Construction Supervisors	94	517
17.	Printing Technology	158	1232
18.	Woodworking and Carpentry	90	414
19.	Office Assistant/Secretaryship	94	790
20.	Counseling and Career Guidance	353	530
21.	Hotel Management	153	680
22.	Beautician and Healthcare	136	291
23.	Advertisement and Journalism	94	291
24.	Fashion Technology	7	28
25.	Engineering	441	3616
Total			**23,944**

Table IX. Chennai At a Glance: Employment and Placement (2001-2005)

S.No	*Areas of Employment*	*Total No. of Units in the area of Employment*	*Total No. of Jobs Up To 2005 AD*
1.	Air-conditioning and Refrigeration	142	909
2.	Automobile Technology	171	992
3.	Beautician and Health Care	76	308
4.	Bakery and Confectionery	80	266
5.	Book Publication	129	548
6.	Computer Software	149	13,306
7.	Computer Hardware	89	1,611
8.	Courier Service	148	4,114
9.	Construction Management	118	3,764
10.	Cargo Management	140	1,414
11.	Electrical and Electronics	93	474
12.	Amusement Parks	4	400
13.	Furniture Making	175	4,228
14.	Hotel and Hospitality Service	396	16,394
15.	Hospital and Allied Services	255	9,626
16.	Interior Decoration	194	2,968
17.	Medical Lab Technician	63	227
18.	Leather Garments and Export	652	34,425
19.	Multi Mechanism	80	2,232
20.	Printing Technology	787	8,027
21.	Commercial Photography	92	478
22.	Retail Sales and Marketing	474	12,324
23.	Pre-School Teacher	344	5,985
24.	Security Management	88	16,773
25.	Travel and Tourism Management	505	6,363
	Total		**1,48,156**

• **Need Analysis booklets preserved at MCRDCE.**

Thanks to the Need Analysis Team that have worked in different parts of the country with MCRDCE, Chennai

4
Curriculum Development

4.1 Introduction

There has been a lot of struggle during the last nine years in discovering the relevant and the needed curriculum to be given to the students of the Community College. So what is offered as the Curriculum taught in the Community Colleges is a result of the collective search and it is based on the actual teaching experience of many of the Community College Teachers.

4.2 The Curriculum of a Community College

The Curriculum of a Community College for a Job Oriented diploma programme

Given below is a suggested course outline:

Duration of the programme is for 52 Weeks and it has 4 distinct parts.

- Depending on the learning level of the target groups in the local areas, the college could conduct classes from the minimum of *three hours* (for part timers) to maximum of *Six Hours* per day. (for full timers).
- The curriculum for every Job-Oriented Programme should be designed in collaboration with the practitioners of the Industry / Commerce / Service Agricultural / Rural Sectors.
- The college should help the students to attain their *Entry-Level Skills* required for the Job-Oriented Programmes.

PART - I LIFE SKILLS			
S. No	*Programme*	*Duration*	*Hours*
1.	Students Orientation	1 Week	30 Hours
2.	Life Coping Skills	6 Weeks	180 Hours
3.	Interpersonal Relationship and Communication Skills	4 Weeks	120 Hours
4.	Developmental English	6 Weeks	180 Hours
5.	Basic Computer Applications	4 Weeks	120 Hours
PART - II WORK SKILLS			
1.	Career Guidance and Counseling	1 Week	30 Hours
2.	Work Skills	20 Weeks	600 Hours
PART - III INTERNSHIP AND HANDS ON EXPERIENCE			
1.	Internship and Hands on Experience	8 Weeks	390 Hours
PART - IV PREPARATION FOR EMPLOYMENT AND EVALUATION			
1.	Preparation for Employment and Evaluation	2 Weeks	60 Hours
Total No. of Weeks and Hours		**52 Weeks**	**1710 Hours**

- For the Certificate Courses, the Life Skills should be compulsory and the duration of the Work Skill Courses could be modified according to the job requirements.
- For all the students of the Community College whatever might be their specialized programmes, *Courses on Life Skills are mandatory.*
- It is advisable to have 25 to 30 students maximum for skills development in specific Job-oriented Programmes.
- The presence of Job Placement Cell and Placement Officer is a must in every Community College for effective internship training and subsequent Job Placement.

4.3 Transfer of Credits towards Vertical Mobility

The Madras Centre for Research and Development of Community Education (MCRDCE), Chennai is making attempts and negotiating with *Indira Gandhi National Open University (IGNOU), New Delhi,* for the Transfer of Credits from the Community College to the University Courses which will help the students of the Community Colleges to integrate themselves into the main stream and facilitate their vertical mobility.

Eg: (i) *Diploma in Nursing Assistant* in a Community College can lead towards the Vertical Mobility to IGNOU Programme – *B.Sc. Nursing* through *Transfer of Credits.*

(ii) *Diploma in Computer Software* in a Community College can lead towards the Vertical Mobility to IGNOU Programme – *B.C.A.* though *Transfer of Credits.*

- These are only suggestions and these need to be formalized.

Suggested Credit System

Part I. Life Skills

S.No	Programme	Duration	Hours	Cred its
1.	Students Orientation	1 Week	30 Hours	1 Credit
2.	Life Coping Skills	6 Weeks	180 Hours	6 Credits
3.	Interpersonal Relationship and Communication Skills	4 Weeks	120 Hours	4 Credits
4.	Developmental English	6 Weeks	180 Hours	6 Credits
5.	Basic Computer Applications	4 Weeks	120 Hours	4 Credits
	TOTAL	**21 Weeks**	**630 Hours**	**21 Credits**

Part II. Work Skills

S.No	Programme	Duration	Hours	Credits
1.	Career Guidance and Counseling	1 Week	30 Hours	1 Credit
2.	Work Skills	20 Weeks	600 Hours	20 Credit
	TOTAL	**21 Weeks**	**630 Hours**	**21 Credit**

Part III. Internship And Hands On Experience

S.No	Programme	Duration	Hours	Credits
1.	Internship and Hands on Experience	8 Weeks	390 Hours	13 Credits
	TOTAL	**8 Weeks**	**390 Hours**	**13 Credits**

Part – IV : Preparation for Employment and Evaluation

S.No	Programme	Duration	Hours	Credits
1.	Preparation for Employment and Evaluation	2 Weeks	60 Hours	2 Credits
	TOTAL	**2 Weeks**	**60 Hours**	**2 Credits**

Total Number of Credits

Category	Programme	Weeks	Hours	Credits
PART I	Life Skills	21 Weeks	630 Hours	21 Credits
PART II	Work Skills	21 Weeks	630 Hours	21 Credits
PART III	Internship and Hands on Experience	8 Weeks	390 Hours	13 Credits
PART IV	Preparation for Employment and Evaluation	2 Weeks	60 Hours	2 Credits
	TOTAL	**52 Weeks**	**1710 Hours**	**57 Credits**

4.4 DACUM Process

The Job-Oriented Programmes for different fields of specialization have to be designed with the collaboration of experts from the fields. They become the members of the advisory boards of the Community Colleges.

The Community Colleges follows the **DACUM** (Developing a Curriculum) with the following stages.

1. The exact Description of the Job – Example – Financial Assistant, Community Development Organiser, Nursing Assistant, Office Assistant, Construction Supervisor.
2. The Responsibilities and tasks the person should fulfill.
3. The Skills required to fulfil these tasks.
4. The courses needed to equip them with the skills.

4.5 Skills Chart "Office Assistant" evolved using the DACUM Process

Skills Required for an Office Assistant

Personal Skills

Punctuality, Pleasing Personality, Sincerity, Loyalty, Responsibility, Reliability, Spontaneity, Ethical, Industrious, Self Esteem, Good Perception , presentability, Stress Management Problem Solving, Presence of Mind, Hard Working.

Social Skills

Acceptability, Listening, patience, Ability to solve Interpersonal Conflicts, Overcoming, Inhibitions, Hospitality, Overcoming Shyness, Accepting One's faults, Handling hardships and failures and Approachability.

Communication Skills

Dialogue, Group Communication, Clarity, Public Speaking, Good Expression, Ability to Understand, Interpretation, Oral and Written, Formal and Informal, Presentation Skills, Presentation of a good curriculum Vitae.

Work Skills

Computing Skills, Handling of Office Automation Products: Xerox, Fax, Record Maintenance, EPBX, Business

Correspondence, Drafting, Typing and Short handling Stationery, Utilisation of Resources Electricity. Cost Consciousness, Office Assistance, Computer Assistance, Accounting Skills, Banking Skills and Awareness of Competitors.

Creative Skills

Updating of Knowledge and Skills, Innovative, Risk Taking, More Imaginative.

Leadership

Empathy, Impartiality, Co-Ordination, Animation, Facilitator, Team Building, Approachability, Dynamic, Crisis Management, Resourcefulness, Focused, Participatory Leadership, Decision Making, Counselling, Service Minded, Initiative, Delegations, Self Motivations, Appreciative, Organisation Skills.

Language Skills

Multilingual

4.6 Curriculum evolved during the Community College Teachers Training Programme, June 2001 using the DACUM Process.

1. Nursing Assistant
2. Tailoring and Embroidery
3. Community Development
4. Multi Mechanic
5. Rural Community Development Worker
6. Hotel Management

Sample-DACUM Process
1. Nursing Assistant

Personal Skills

Checking the Vital Signs, Transferring the patient from place to place, administering the medicine, Attentive to the patient, controlling the disturbance from the visitors, Punctuality, Self Control, Taking Care of Patients in Emergency, dressing and cleaning, sterilization procedure, Lab text, Taking care of child health, Family Health, Carry out the Instructions of Doctors and Nurses.

Social Skills

Kind, Sympathetic, Hope, Giving, Duty Conscious, Commitment, Pleasant, Understanding, Affectionate.

Work Skills

Neatness, Self-Hygiene, Confidently, discharging the duty, Presence of Mind, Hospitality, Service Minded, Hard Working.

Courses Required

- Anatomy and Physiology
- Microbiology
- Communicable Disease
- Mental Health
- First Aid
- Nutrition
- Maternity and Child Care
- Fundamentals of Nursing
- Preventive Medicine
- Study of Human Body
- Communication Skills
- Counselling
- Behavioural Approach
- Works Skills
- Interpersonal Relationship
- Human Relationship and Team Work

2. Tailoring and Embroidery

Personal Skills

Perfection Stitching, Punctuality, Sincerity, Time Management, learning New Models and designs, Pleasing Personality, Good Relationship, Hard Working, Involvement.

Communication Skills

Multilingual Skills, Approachability.

Work Skills

Perfection in stitching, Developing variety of designs, thorough knowledge.

Creative Skills

Updating of Knowledge and Skills.

Mechanical Skills

Repairing and Maintenance.

Selection Skills

Colour Matching, Thread Selection, Needle Selection.

Courses Skills

Computer Pattern Making, Tailoring and Embroidery, Garment Quality Control, Garment Export Management.

3. Community Development

Personal Skills

Pleasing, Kindness, hard Working, Problem Solving, Presence of Mind, Responsibility, Self Esteem, Impartial, Confidentiality.

Communication Skills

Interaction and Dialogue, Understanding capacity, Oral Communication, Creating awareness, Public Speaking.

Responsibility

Understanding the vision of the Agencies, Ready to work anywhere and at anytime, Accountability to the Agencies and to the Community, Ensuring people's participation in their decision-making, working and role model.

Work Skills

Preparing Project Proposal, Problem Solving, Handling of the Community, Counselling Mediation Skills, Utilising Local Skills Developmental Skills.

Courses Required

Basic Social Work Concept, Social Analysis, Community Welfare programme, Social Work Methods, Basic Psychology, Group Dynamics.

Job Description

Developing officer, Field Worker, Target People, Social Change, Field Visits and Building Rapport, Identifying Local

Leaders and Resources, Local Needs, Organising the Local Community, Conducting Periodical Meetings, Case Study, Survey, Monitoring of Programme.

4. Multi Mechanic

Personal Skills

Responsibility and Hardwork Industrious, Practice, Ethics, Punctuality and Sincerity, Problem Solving, presence of mind and good perception, Loyalty.

Social Skills

Listening Skills, Acceptability, Solving Interpersonal problems, Quality of network.

Communication Skills

Multilingual, Good Expression, Understanding.

Work Skills

- Electrical
- Electronics
- Carpentry
- Mechanical
- Plumbing.

Creative Skills

- Innovative
- Risk Taking
- Imaginative
- Updating of Skills.

Leadership

- Resourcefulness
- Approachability
- Decision Making
- Service Minded
- Organisation Skills.

Mechanic

Identification of Tools and there usage in homes and flats. Eg: Hammer, Screw Driver, Jumper, Fill-Drilling, Machine, Cutting Player.

Masonry

Patch up work in house hold, fixing slab, usage of tools – Mixing proportion of Cement and sand and Water – leveling – White Washing – painting – Flooring – Fixing Tiles.

Plumbing

Basic Plumbing ideas and handling of instrument. Repairing and fixing new apparatus in the flats. Knowledge of pipes – quality, diameter, thickness, threading.

Electrical

Wiring Circuits – basic electrical tools and their wages, basic electrical theory – AC DC Current, Basic study of meters – general pre cautions, repairing home appliances, e.g., Refrigeration and T.V.

Carpentry

Fixing Home Furniture, Windows and maintenance. Identifying different type of wood – designing – carving – usage of tools – knowledge of paints – varnish – polishing.

5. Rural Community Development Worker
Responsibility and Tasks

- Conducting survey of the villages and collection of data.
- Problems and the needs identification
- Creating awareness of the causes of the problems.
- Educating them towards group formation organizing them into groups like self-help groups, Women's Association, Youth Club Dairy, Co-operation Societies, Workers Co-operative.
- Educating the rural poor on community health like personal health and hygiene, environmental cleanliness, safe drinking water, mother and child health care.
- Facilitating income-generating programmes.

- Developing saving habits, arranging bank loans, arranging government subsidies.
- Arrange skill-based training like tailoring and embroidery.

Personal Skills

Dedicated, Hard Working, Flexible, Sincerity, Ethical values.

Social Skills

Reaching out, understanding the needs, problem solving skills, hospitality, listening, approachability, impartial, willingness to face challenges, enable people's participation.

Communication Skills

Being relevant, politeness, emphasizing on important convictions, voicing for the voiceless, precise and lively.

Work Skills

Active, alert, awareness of situation, identifying the needs, motivating, prioritizing the implementing efforts, guiding.

Creative Skills

Implementing new techniques according to the changes, innovative schemes, responding to new inspirations and ideas, renovating and modifying traditional methods.

Leadership Skills

Democratic, service minded, co-ordinating, facilitating.

6. Hotel Management

Job Description

Reception, accounting information, travel desk, store keeping, linen maintenance, washing linen / uniforms.

Responsibilities

Handling of Telephone Calls, Guest Relationship, Bill preparation and payments, maintaining records and folios, basic tailoring / stitching, maintenance of linen / uniforms, handling travel desk.

Personal Skills

Responsibilities, hardworking, Pleasing Personality, Problem Solving, Honesty, Loyalty, Enthusiastic, Self-Confidence, Punctuality, memory Power, Good manners, Presence of Mind, Hygienic and Appearance.

Social Skills

- Hospitality
- Approachability
- Courageous
- Patience
- Understanding
- Sociable
- Gentleness
- Kindness.

Communication Skills

Interpretation, Diplomatic and Expressive.

Creative Skills

Risk Taking, Innovative, Imaginative, Decoration of the Hotel.

Work Skills

Computing Skills, Knowledge of the locality, Foreign Exchange, Time table of Airways, Roadways and Railways.

Leadership Skills

Co-ordination, Decision Making, Planning, Dynamic, Team Building, Counselling, Impartiality, Initiative.

4.7 Curriculum evolved during the Community College Teachers Training Programme, November 2001 using the DACUM Process.

1. Pre School Training

Advisory Board

Child Psychologist, Parents, faculty, head Master of the School, Child, Specialist, Director of the Community College, Professional Social Worker, Child Specialist.

Job Description

Task and Responsibilities

Impartiality, Kindness, Loving, Motherly, Child Psychologist, Understanding, Model Teacher. Personal Skills.

Lovable, Hard Working, Problem Solving, Responsibility, Presence of mind, Practice Ethics, Hard Working, Listening, Creativity, Approachability.

Social Skills

Facing hardship, Listening, Patience, Acceptance and Approachability.

Work Skills

Maintaining Play toys, chart making, maintaining records, clay modeling, resource utilization, cleanliness, social awareness, sense of humour, presence of mind.

Communication Skills

Effective Order, Pronunciation, Good Expression, Intonation.

Leadership

Impartial, Appreciation, Acceptance, Crisis Management, Service Mindedness, Facilitator.

Creative Skills

Innovation, Singing, Story telling, body language, drawing, imagination, colouring.

Courses to be Given

Teaching of the Alphabets, Identifying the given picture, clay modeling, child development, story telling.

2. Tailoring and Embroidery

Advisory Board

Fashion Designers, Popular and Experienced tailors, Embroiders, Principal of the Community College.

Tasks and Responsibility

Exact Measurement, Creativity, Knowledge of the latest design, garments, knowledge of the latest machinery, technical knowledge, customers satisfaction, time management, material management, maintenance of the situated design.

Personal Skills

Patience, Punctuality, Sincerity, Loyalty, hard Working, Practices, Ethics, Self Esteem, Innovative, Keen observation, good eyesight.

Leadership

Resourcefulness, self motivation, role model.

Creative Sills

Imaginative, Dynamic, Innvative, Artistic.

Communication Skills

Perception, Oral Communication, Clarity, Convincing.

Work

Awareness of Competition, Designing, Embroidery, Accountability, Measruing, Accuracy, Pattern Making, Drafting, Utlisation of resources.

Social Skills

Appreciation, Eager to learn, Hospitality, Humility, Sacrifice.

3. Nursing Assistant

Personal Skills

Punctuality, Pleasing Personality, Sincerity, Loyalty, Responsibility, Reliability, Problem Solving, presence of Mind, Hard Working, Good Perception, Commitment.

Social Skills

Hospitality, Patience, Listening, Acceptability, Overcoming Inhibitions, Accepting one's own faults, approachability, overcoming shyness, handling hardships and failures, solving interpersonal conflicts.

Communication Skills

Dialogue, Oral and Written, Presentation Skills, Group Communication, Clarity, Public Speaking, Good Expression, Ability to understand, interpretation.

Language Skills

Multi lingual, well versed in the regional language.

Creative Skills

Updating of knowledge and skills, innovative, risk taking.

Leadership Skills

Resourcefulness, Dynamic, Impartiality, Empathy, Co-ordination Facilitator, Team Building, Approachability, Crisis Management, Focused, Decision Making, Counseling, Service Mindedness, Initiative, Delegation, Self Motivation, Appreciative, Organisation Skills.

Work Skills

Hygiene, Basic Nursing Skills, Observing and reporting, Utilization of resources and equipments, assisting the nurse, developing interpersonal relations, awareness towards environmental sanitation, knowledge about legal aspects, maternity and delivery identifying and treating of emergency cases. inability, Problem Solving, presence of Mind, Hard Working, Good Perception, Commitment.

4. Hotel Management

Personal Skills

Punctuality, Pleasing Personality, Sincerity, Loyalty, Presence of Mind, Hard Working, Industrious, self-esteem, good perception, discipline, sense of humour.

Social Skills

Acceptability, patience, Listening, Hospitality, Overcoming, shyness, accepting faults, handling hardships and failures, approachability, sacrifice for the team, risk taking, decision making.

Leadership Skills

Empathy, Impartiality, Co-ordination, Animation Team Building, Dynamic, facilitator, Crisis Management, Counseling, ervice Mindedness, Initiative, Self Motivation.

Communication Skills

Dialogue, Oral and Written, presentation Skills, Communication Skills, Public Speaking, Good Expression, Ability to understand.

Creative Skills

Innovative, Risk Taking, More Imaginative, Carving vegetables, bakery models.

Work Skills

Assistant Receptionist, Bell boy, House Keeping, Waiter, Assistant Cook.

Language Skills

Multi Lingual

5. Computer Software

Job Description

To prepare the candidates to becomes a Data Entry Operator as well as to provide the Basic Skills required to operate a Computer.

Responsibilities and Duties

Knowledge of the Operating System, Packages, Accuracy of Performance, Drafting, preparing of Official Correspondence, Knowledge of operating the printer, knowledge of the latest applications – Internet Browsing, Creating E-mail ID and sending mails, Using Computers to perform arithmetical calculations, Preparation of charts and reports, ability to draw, knowledge of loading and correcting minor problems.

Personal Job Description

Punctuality, Pleasing Personality, Sincerity, Loyalty, Responsibility, reliability-Mental and Physical, Concentration, Spontaneity, Problem Solving, Presence of Mind, Hard Working, Industrious, self-esteem, good perception.

Social Skills

Acceptability, Listening, Patience, Solving Interpersonal Conflicts, Overcoming Inhibitions and Shyness, Accepting one's own faults, handling hardships and failures and approachability.

Communication Skills

Oral and Written, presentation Skills, Group Communication Good Reports, Clarity, Ability to understand formal and Informal

Leadership Skills

Empathy, Impartiality, Co-ordination, Animation, Facilitation, Team Building, Dynamic, Approachability, Dynamism, Crisis Management, Resourcefulness, Focused, Participatpry Leadership, Decision Making, Counselling, Service Mindedness, Delegation, Self Motivated, Appreciative, Organisation Skills.

Creative Skills

Updating of Knowledge and Skills, Innovative, Risk taking, More imaginative.

6. Beautician and Healthcare
Work Skills

Handling the equipment, business correspondence, stationery, Utilization of Resources – cost consciousness, office assistant, accounting skills, basic skills, banking skills, awareness of competitors, handling of office automation, record maintenance, handling the clients, observation, time keeping.

Leadership Skills

Empathy, Impartiality, Co-ordination, facilitation, Team Building, Approachability, Dynamic, Crisis Management, Resourcefulness, Decision Making, Service Mindedness, Delegation, Self Motivation, Appreciation, organisation Skills.

Creative Skills

Updating of Knowledge and skills, innovative, risk taking, more imaginative and awareness on beauty.

Communication Skills

Dialogue, Oral and Written, Formal and Informal, presentation Skills, Public Speaking, Ability to Understand.

Social Skills

Acceptability, Listening, patience, Solving Interpersonal Problems, Hospitality, Overcoming Shyness, Accepting one's own faults, handling Hardships and failures, Approachability.

Personal Skills

Punctuality, Pleasing Personality, Sincerity, Loyalty, Spontaneity, problem Solving, Presence of Mind, Hard Working, Self Esteem, Good Perception, presentation Skills, Concentration, Good Dressing.

Job Description

Responsibility, careful Attendance, Profile of every clients, they must have the relationship with other beauticians to update themselves.

Language Skills

Multi Lingual.

5
Life Skills

5.1 Life Coping Skills

1. Introduction

Coping is the effort we make to manage situations we experience as potentially harmful or stressful. A coping attitude is a philosophy that says life will not always be the way we want it to be, but our coping skills can help us make the best of it.

2. The Objectives of the Programme

To enrich the lives of young adults

(a) By understanding the meaning of life and its challenges.

(b) By providing skills and knowledge needed to cope with life's problems and challenges.

(c) By developing a positive attitude towards themselves in this process.

(d) By assisting in being successful and useful citizens.

The programme will consider coping responses we already know and the ones we don't know and want to learn. We will understand that human beings are adaptable and the ability to cope is developed and perfected throughout one's life.

The programme will conclude by discussing coping as a life philosophy. At the end of the course the students will be encouraged to become well rounded persons with strong and positive coping skills to meet a challenging and unpredictable and competitive world.

3. Course Outline

Part I Developing Personal Skills

Unit 1	Introduction and outline of the Programme, Meaning and Explanation of Coping, Positive and Negative Mechanisms of Coping
Unit 2	Restructuring one's own Life Story, Positive and Negative Messages
Unit 3	Self Esteem, Self-Concept, Self-Acceptance and Personality Development
Unit 4	Positive Thinking
Unit 5	Motivation and Self- Actualisation
Unit 6	Goal Setting
Unit 7	Meaning and Attitude to Success
Unit 8	Problem Solving
Unit 9	Decision Making
Unit 10	Time- Management
Unit 11	Stress Management

Part II Developing Coping Mechanisms

Unit 12	Coping with Human Sexuality
Unit 13	Coping with Shyness
Unit 14	Coping with Loneliness
Unit 15	Coping with Depression
Unit 16	Coping with Fear
Unit 17	Coping with Anger and Verbal Abuse
Unit 18	Coping with HIV AIDS
Unit 19	Coping with Alcoholism and Substance Abuse
Unit 20	Coping with Failure
Unit 21	Coping with Criticism
Unit 22	Coping with Conflict
Unit 23	Coping with Change
Unit 24	Coping with Study

Part III Developing Fitness for a Job

Unit 25 Leadership

Unit 26 Team Work

Unit 27 Career Guidance

Unit 28 Work Environment

4. The Description of the Unit

Unit–1 Introduction and outline of the Programme, Meaning and Explanation of Coping, Positive and Negative Mechanisms of Coping

The students are taught the meaning of coping, the coping process and the mechanisms of coping both positive and negative. The issues concerning them and the problem situations faced by them are dealt with at length. They are made to realize that it is better to develop healthy, acceptable, honest mechanisms to face the challenges of life.

Unit–2 Restructuring one's own Life Story, Positive and Negative Messages

The students are made to understand the influences both internal and external affecting the human perception, their attitude to it and their behaviour patterns, in response to these influences.

Unit–3 Self Esteem, Self Concept, Self Acceptance and Personality Development

The concept of self esteem is explained and the students are made to understand why self esteem is important for a person and how it can help them in the task of positive self development. They are taught to accept themselves as they are with all their strengths and weaknesses so that it can lead them to live as fuller and richer persons, fully alive and human.

Unit–4 Positive Thinking

To help the students to have the right perception of life. To emphasize the good in their lives, to transform them from soft and tender minded to tough minded individuals, from weak, negative individuals to men and women of strength.

Unit–5 Motivation and Self Actualisation

To explain the concept of motivation and to say how it is linked with energizing and directing their efforts toward a meaningful goal. To help them understand that enhancing their motivation involves becoming more self-directed, that is performing out of their own needs, desires and aspirations.

Unit–6 Goal Setting

To familiarize them with the different types of goals, the importance of the pursuit of personal goals and setting goals and striving to reach them.

Unit–7 Meaning and Attitude to Success

Success is part and parcel of one's life. It has an element of unpredictability and also perfect satisfaction with oneself and one's achievements. It is important that proper attitude to success is developed by the students. This attitude is being taught through theoretical input and exercises.

Unit–8 Problem Solving

Helping students to see their problems in terms of their past decisions, to examine the consequences of such decisions and then choose a more satisfying alternative.

Unit–9 Decision Making

The students should learn to view their problems in terms of their decisions than as a result of events and circumstances that simply happen. Help them understand that decisions are especially crucial with regard to personal growth.

Unit–10 Time Management

To tell the students about the importance of time in their lives, the judicious use of time and how if used effectively can help them achieve their goals.

Unit–11 Stress Management

Students learn how to manage stress – including the intense emotions aroused in a more appropriate manner. They learn to take charge, directing and controlling their responses to stress inorder to modify the overall stress situations and meet physical challenges, solve problems and reach goals.

Unit–12 Coping with Human Sexuality

The students are familiarized with the different stages of the human life cycle from birth to death. They are also made to understand that in addition to biological changes, environmental factors shape adolescents and their social development in ways that influence their behaviour in adulthood and to have a proper perspective and attitudes towards sexuality.

Unit–13 Coping with Shyness

To understand the meaning of shyness and the ways and means to overcome the same.

Unit–14 Coping with Loneliness

Help them interpret loneliness as changeable or learning to like themselves by using solitude for pursuing self-fulfilling activities.

Unit–15 Coping with Depression

To understand the meaning and nature of depression, symptoms of depression and the causes for depression and also the ways to overcome depression.

Unit–16 Coping with Fear

The common feature of life is fear of all kinds. How to understand the various kinds of fear and how to handle fear and overcome the same.

Unit–17 Coping with Anger and Verbal Abuse

Help the students understand that anger is a common reaction to frustration and mistreatment and that they are all destined to face occasions causing anger throughout their lives but it must be dealt with otherwise it can hinder them from reaching their goals.

Unit–18 Coping with HIV AIDS

To understand the burning problem of AIDS and its grave consequences and the facts on HIV, stages of HIV AIDS, infection symptoms and transmission of AIDS, Treatment of AIDS and approaching with compassion HIV affected persons.

Unit–19 Coping with Alcoholism and Substance Abuse

To perceive the evils of alcoholism and the ways it could be treated and also the ways of coping with drugs and helping drug addicts.

Unit–20 Coping with Failure

To help them understand that failure is not a positive experience but that they should take it in their stride. They should accept experiences of failure as part of life and to save their energy for coping with failures that they honestly feel are worthy getting upset about.

Unit–21 Coping with Criticism

Criticism is an inevitable reality in our life. The students are introduced to different kinds of criticism and the ways of handling them. They are given an idea of giving and receiving criticism.

Unit–22 Coping with Conflict

To understand conflict is a fact of life and to have a distinction between constructive and destructive conflict and also the strategies to manage conflict.

Unit–23 Coping with Change

- Developing the right attitude towards change that is inevitable in life.
- Developing the coping mechanism to various changes that take place in our life.

- Developing the attitude of flexibility to adjust oneself to fact of change.

Unit–24 Coping with Study

Explaining to the students that study is the most important part of their curriculum and if dealt with methodically can become a pleasure and help them excel in their academics.

Unit–25 Leadership

- To understand the nature and types of leadership
- To enumerate the characteristics of good leadership
- To take on the leadership role where ever it is necessary with courage and confidence.

Unit–26 Team Work

- To introduce the students, the dynamics and working of the team.
- To understand the ways and means of team building.
- To imbibe the skills of working as a member of a team.

Unit–27 Career Guidance

- To introduce the students that there is a variety of careers from which one can choose.
- There are various factors one has to consider before choosing a career.
- And how to choose a career that suite them.

Unit–28 Work Environment

- Understanding the nature of the work environment.
- Knowing the qualities and characteristics required to create a favourable and healthy work environment.
- How to build a better work environment.

5. The Plan of the Programme

- The duration of the Programme will be for 6 Weeks. Each

unit will be handled for 6 Hours. The total number of hours will be 28 x 6 = 168hours.

- The structure of every unit will be the following with the time allotted.
- Evaluation for 12 Hours
  - **One Credit = 30 Hours of Work**

Programme	*Duration*	*Hours*	*Credits*
Life Coping Skills	6 Weeks	180 Hours	6 Credits

1. **Learning Objective and Brainstorming Session** – To explain to the students what is going to be done and why. A question relevant to the subject dealt with is asked and answers are elicited from the students. – 2 hours
2. **Theoretical Input** – 2 Hours
3. Exercises and Group Activity – 1½ Hours
4. The summary of the Unit is done by the students – ½ Hour each Unit will be handled for 6 Hours in 2 Sessions of 3 Hours each.

You are encouraged to use transparencies, posters, group discussion, role play, questionnaire and all other possible means of activity to make every Unit *totally an interactive session.*

There are charts and questionnaires given as exercises. The scores are also given by which the students can make an assessment of that particular subject. The teachers are asked not to reveal the scores when they administer the questionnaire to the students.

6. Methodology and Evaluation

1. Explanation of the theme and input
2. Games and Role Plays to elicit the relevant points from the students
3. Questionnaires for assessment
4. Guest lectures by experts in specific fields
5. Presentation by students 3-5 minutes on the benefits of the programme.

6. Assignment
7. Written test : Objective and Essay Types
8. Group Discussion
9. Poster Exhibition.

Evaluation of Life Skill Programme in Community Colleges

Life Skills

Life Coping Skills		
1.	Assignments	4 x 5 = 20 marks
2.	Two Tests	2 x 5 = 10 marks
3.	Oral Presentation	10 marks
4.	Group Discussion	10 marks
5.	Poster Presentation	10 marks
6.	Final Examination	40 marks
	Total	**100 marks**

Skills Assessment Chart : **Shows the greater emphasis given to Life Coping Skills in the assessment of the student by the Internship Supervisor.**

Name : ____________________

Job Oriented Programme : ____________________

Place of Training : ____________________

Campus Admitted : ____________________

Please Rate the following skills by a Tick Mark

5 – Excellent; 4 – Very Good; 3 – Above Average; 2 – Average and 1 – Poor.

- **The rating of workskills is also added.**

7. Since the Life Coping Skills Programme will bring up many issues and problems of students, *personal counseling* is very much recommended for the students.
8. It is also important to prepare a profile of a student done at the entry level, mid term course level and exit level.

S. No	Personal Skills	5	4	3	2	1
1.	Punctuality					
2.	Sincerity					
3.	Self-Esteem					
4.	Responsibility					
5.	Reliability					
6.	Spontaneity					
7.	Problem Solving					
8.	Presence of Mind					
9.	Hard Working					
10.	Stress Management					
S. No	**Social Skills**	**5**	**4**	**3**	**2**	**1**
1.	Listening					
2.	Patience					
3.	Hospitality					
4.	Overcoming Shyness					
5.	Accepting one's own fault's					
S. No	**Communication Skills**	**5**	**4**	**3**	**2**	**1**
1.	Dialogue					
2.	Oral and Written					
3.	Presentation Skills					
4.	Good Expression					
5.	Ability to understand					
S. No	**Language Skills**	**5**	**4**	**3**	**2**	**1**
1.	Multilingual					
2.	Speaking					
3.	Writing					
S. No	**Creative Skills**	**5**	**4**	**3**	**2**	**1**
1.	Updating of Skills					
2.	Innovative					
3.	Risk Taking					
4.	Imaginative					
5.	Industrious					
6.	Other talents (singing, dancing etc)					

S. No	Leadership Skills	5	4	3	2	1
1.	Empathy					
2.	Impartiality					
3.	Coordination					
4.	Animation					
5.	Team Building					
6.	Approachability					
7.	Dynamic					
8.	Resourcefulness					
9.	Initiative					
10.	Organisation Skills					

The format of the profile file would be the following :

1. Name of the student with all his / her details
2. Family Background
3. Income
4. Strengths

5. Handicaps of the students
6. The improvements taking place
7. The skills learnt by the student

- *It is also recommended that the students have a class work note book of Life Coping Skills diary in which they record, the entire learning process after every unit and also the answers and fruits of every unit.*
- *Evaluation of the student will be done at the end of every Unit.*

5.2 Interpersonal Relationship and Communication Skills

1. Introduction

Interpersonal Relations and Communication Skills is the sequel to the Life Coping Skills Programme of the Community Colleges. While the Life Coping Skills aim at the development of the personality in terms of sharpening personal skills, learning coping mechanisms and making oneself fit for a job and work environment, the course on Interpersonal Relations at the Community Colleges aims at empowering the student to express and articulate his / her ideas, opinions and to talk about oneself boldly before the interview board and to participate in group discussion and also to speak in public with confidence.

2. The Objectives of the Course

1. To enable the students to become aware of the communication process in their personal and career spheres as well as kinds of communication.
2. To explain to them various interpersonal skills needed in their day-to-day interaction with others.
3. To enable students to achieve oral fluency on various dimensions of communicative competence in English.
4. To learn the art of communicating effectively (i.e.) to express what one feels without offending the feeling of others.
5. To realize the need for having realistic expectations in life especially in interpersonal communication.

6. To train the students in making statements that are descriptive.
7. To help the students to code and decode effectively.
8. To train the students to use communication aids and to avoid communication blocks.
9. To help the students take active part in group discussion.
10. To make the students to become aware of the need for listening.
11. To train the students in public speaking.
12. To train the students in situational language skills and appropriate conversational skills.

3. Focus of the Course

1. Speaking effectively (using feed back, verbal and non-verbal communication)
2. Speaking efficiently (using minimum time with maximum results)
3. Speaking convincingly (a sense of emotional maturity and power)
4. Speaking imperatively (you make the listener accept what you say)
5. Speaking frequently (to speak without any fear or hesitation)

4. Course Outline

Part–I Introduction and Outline of the Programme

Unit–1 Introduction and Outline of the Programme

Part–II Communication in General

Unit–2 The Meaning and Process of Communication

Part–III Interpersonal Communication

Unit–3 Interpersonal Communication

Unit–4 Effective Communication

Unit–5 Situational Language

Unit–6 Expectations in Communication

Unit–7 The Art of Describing and evaluating behaviour

Unit–8 The Art of Coding and Decoding

Unit–9 Communication Aids and Blocks

Part–IV Group Communication

Unit–10 Group Discussion

Unit–11 Public Speaking and Just a Minute

Unit–12 Leadership Communication

Unit–13 Team Communication

Part–V Interpersonal Relationship

Unit–14 Winning at Human Relations

Part–VI Other Communication Skills

Unit–15 Interview Skills

Unit–16 Presentation Skills

Unit–17 Evaluating Communication Skills

5. The Description of the Unit

Unit–1 Introduction and Outline of the Programme

Overview of the course – objectives – areas covered – Focus of the Course

Unit–2 The Meaning and Process of Communication

The Meaning and Process of Communication. Types of communication. Interpersonal skill. Elements of Communication.

Unit–3 Interpersonal Communication

The Skills of Interpersonal Communication. Communication as a skilled behaviour

Unit–4 Effective Communication

Effective Communication. Guidelines for Effective Communication

Unit–5 Situational Language

Greetings, Introduction, Inviting Someone, Making requests, Offering help and assistance, Seeking Permission, Asking for Advice, Expressing Gratitude, Asking about remembering, Persuasion, Complimenting and Congratulating, Expressing Sympathy and Condolence, Complaining, Apologizing, Making Suggestions, Warning Someone, Ending a Conversation, Asking for Information, Asking for Someone's Opinion, Asking for Excuse, Asking Someone to Say Something Again, Checking whether someone has understood you, Asking whether someone knows, Asking about preference, Requesting someone if it is possible to do something, Asking if someone agrees, Asking if you are obliged to do something, Describing something, Some useful expressions.

Unit–6 Expectations in Communication

To realize the need for having realistic expectations in life and in communication because communication breaks down because of 'unrealistic' or 'great' expectations.

Unit–7 The Art of Describing and evaluating behaviour

To train the students in making statements that are descriptive.

Unit–8 The Art of Coding and Decoding

To help the students to code and decode efficiently. The need for proper coding and decoding. Translating an idea into words is a difficult process. Similarly, understanding what one means (not what one says) is equally difficult. Hence one must have the skill to code and decode correctly, otherwise communication fails (I write this letter because I have nothing to do and end this letter because I have nothing to say). Therefore, effective communication is coding and decoding.

Unit–9 Communication Aids and Blocks

- To help the students to use communication AIDS and to avoid communication BLOCKS.

- Communication succeeds when we use responses which build relationships and strengthen communication.
- Communication fails when responses are given that destroy communication and relationship as blocks.

Unit–10 Group Discussion

- How to interact with one another
- Presenting yourself to others
- To improve group communication

Unit–11 Public Speaking and Just a Minute

- The Aims of Public Speaking
- The manner of public speaking
- The Characteristic need for public speaking

Unit–12 Leadership Communication

- To describe the different types of Leadership Communication

Unit–13 Team Communication

- Learn to value the strength of others
- To develop team work
- Improve communication skills

Unit–14 Winning at Human Relations

- Inculcating in the minds of students the important role interpersonal relationships play in the process of personality development.
- Helping students develop and maintain caring and productive relationships within the family and among friends.

Unit–15 Interview Skills

To make students fit for an interview.

Unit–16 Presentation Skills

To make an effective presentation

Unit–17 Evaluating Communication Skills

6. Evaluation of the Course

The course lasts for 4 weeks with 120 hours. It is a course for 4 Credits. One Credit is 30 Hours of work.

Each unit has a following outline.

1. Learning Objectives
2. Brainstorming Session (Wherever it is necessary)
3. Theoretical Input
4. Exercises – individual and group (Wherever it is necessary)

7. The Scheme of Evaluation

So the entire course aims at improving and sharpening the speaking, listening and communicating skills of the students. The modest outcome of the programme is that the students are able to speak atleast 15 sentences in English. He / She is able to do the same before an interview board. Hence it is recommended that it is more practice of actual communication exercises in classes needed and necessary rather than an undue emphasis on the theoretical part of the programme. It is earnestly recommended that we have 60% of the practical and 40% of theory.

Interpersonal Relations and Communication Skills			
1.	Two Assignments	10 x 5 =	20 marks
2.	Two Tests	5 x 2 =	10 marks
3.	Group Discussion		10 marks
4.	Public Speaking		10 marks
5.	Just a Minute		10 marks
6.	Final Examination		40 marks
		Total	**100 marks**

5.3 Basic Computer Applications

1. Introduction

Basic Computer Applications course is designed to provide the basic elementary and computing skills for the disadvantaged students who cannot afford to pay the fees charged by the private institutions. This course will train the students on Computer Fundamentals, MS –Word, Excel, Power Point, DeskTop Publishing and Computer Maintenance. Basic Computer Applications will help the students of the community colleges to work independently and accurately.

2. Objectives

1. The student will get the information about the world of Personal Computer.
2. To train the students on the basic concept on Hardware and Software.
3. It provides the necessary skills to operate and maintain a Personal Computer.
4. To train the students on Formatting text and Printing
5. To provide the skills about the integration of Data Management, facilities from different software packages.
6. To develop basic elementary and computing skills.

3. Course Outline

Part–I Introduction to Computer

Unit–1 Introduction to Computer

Unit–2 Computer Architecture and Organisation

Unit–3 Peripheral Devices

Unit–4 Computer Software

Part–II Operating System

Unit–5 Disk Operating System

Part–III Office Automation

Unit–6 Office Automation

Unit–7 MS Word

Unit–8 Working with Text

Unit–9 Working with Tables, Graphics and Pages

Unit–10 Mail Merge

Part–IV MS Excel

Unit–11 MS Excel

Part–V MS PowerPoint

Unit–12 MS PowerPoint

Part–VI MS Access

Unit–13 MS Access

Part–VII MS Outlook

Unit–14 MS Outlook

Part–VIII Internet

Unit–15 Internet and Email

4. Evaluation and Assessment - Weightage

On going assessment

- The entire evaluation - ongoing assessment (40%) Theory and (60%) Practical will be conducted by the institution internally.

Eligibility Criteria

Class Attendance and work 80%

Pass Criteria

40% On going Assessment

40% Practical

A. Theory	*80 Marks*	
a. Assignment		10 Marks
b. Seminar		10 Marks
c. Tests	(6x5)	30 Marks
d. Final Examination		30 Marks
	Total Marks	**80 Marks**

B. Practical	*120 Marks*	
a. Six Tests	6x10	60 Marks
b. Final Examination		60 Marks
	Total	**120 Marks**

5.4 Developmental English

1. Introduction

Language is a means of communication that promotes order and harmony in the society. English is a language, which makes communication easy at the global level. It also enables dissemination of ideas, ideologies, inventions and new practices faster among various countries. Coming to our country there is no common language, which can connect all the states except English. Hence knowledge in English has become an essential need in the field of trade and commerce, industry and service sectors. Increasingly it is becoming important due to the modern technology in which English is being used globally.

Acquiring command over the language makes easy not only communication, but also to build up relationship faster and promotes self-confidence. Knowledge and capacity to speak English has become the pre-requisite for job-opportunity in every field. Therefore, importance is attached to train the students of community colleges to acquire English knowledge and to improve their spoken English.

2. Objectives

(a) To help the students learn the structure of English Grammar.

(b) To improve the level of listening and reading skills.

(c) To motivate the student to understand the need for communication and language skills (English) in their daily lives.

(d) To increase their vocabulary and enable them to communicate effectively in various situations, by enhancing their speaking and writing skills.

(e) To increase the functional competence of the students in English language skills in various environments – At home, class, work, social events and other day to day events.

(f) To develop linguistic skills in the English language.

3. Preparation for the Job

1. Developmental English will help the students to prepare a good bio-data.
2. The students can speak fluently in English in their work places.
3. Writing skills will help the students to communicate effectively in their work place.

4. The Content of the Course

Part–I	Basic Grammar
Part–II	Formation of Sentences
Part–III	Correction of Common Errors in English
Part–IV	Increasing the Word Power
Part–V	Development of story with Hints
Part–VI	Comprehension
Part–VII	Paragraph Writing
Part–VIII	Letter Writing
Part–IX	Newspaper Clippings
Part–X	Precise Writing
Part–XI	Preparation of Bio-Data
Part–XII	Essay Writing

Duration

Developmental English 6 Weeks = 30 Hours per week = 180 Hours = 6 Credits

Format of Study

Section	*Topic*	*Theory*	*Practical*	*Total*
A	Grammar and Vocabulary	24	36	60
B	Reading and Listening	12	18	30
C	Conversation and Dialogue	16	24	40
D	Writing Skills	20	30	50
	Total	72	108	180

Evaluation And Assessment - Weightage

On going assessment	
a. Ten Letters and Ten Paragraphs Writing	= 10 Marks
b. 20 Exercises (News Paper Clippings)	= 10 Marks
c. 20 categories (Flowers, Towns etc)	= 10 Marks
d. 200 Words from the Dictionary	= 10 Marks
e. Two Tests	= 20 Marks
Total	**60 Marks**
(f) **Final Examination**	**40 Marks**
Total Marks	**100 Marks****

- The entire evaluation - ongoing assessment (60%) and final exam (40%) will be conducted by the institution internally.

Eligibility Criteria

Class Attendance and work 80%

Pass Criteria

Internal 40 %

External 40%

6
Work Skills

6.1 The Possible Programmes that could be conducted in the Community Colleges based on the Need Analysis.

(1) Health

Medical Lab Technician, Theatre Assistant, Pharmacy Assistant, Medical records Clerk, Physician's Office Assistant, Radiology Assistant, X-Ray Assistant, CT Scan, Ward Assistant, Nursing Assistant (general), Nursing Assistant (Intensive Care), Midwife First Reporter (Emergency Medicine), Technician (Emergency Medicine), Paramedical Assistant, Siddha Ayurvedic Herbal and Nature Medicine.

(2) Rural Development

Community Development and Health Worker, Pre School Teacher, Rural Marketing, Alternative Tourism.

(3) Agriculture

Multi Purpose Farm Supervising, Dairy Farming, Seed Technology, Horticulture, Plantations Management, Organic farming, Dry farming.

(4) Technical

Construction Management, Four Wheeler Mechanism, Two Wheeler Mechanism, Diesel Technology, Printing Technology, Multi Mechanic Skills, Computer Software and Hardware Technology, Commercial Photography, Tiles Manufacturing

Technology, Visual and Graphics Mixing, Air Conditioning and Refrigeration, Home Appliances Service and Maintenance, Interior Decoration.

(5) Non-Technical

Shipping (Cargo) management, Sales and Marketing Management, Office Accountant and Secretaryship, Security Service, Transport Fleet Management, Advertisement, Aqua Culture, Bakery and Confectionery, Beautician and Health Care, Book Publishing and Selling, Courier Services, Export Garments Manufacturing, Fashion Designing, Hotel Management and Hospitality Services, Journalism, Soft and Hot Beverage Manufacturing, Travel and Tourism Operations.

(6) Self Employment and Small Business Development

Other job-oriented programmes could be added according to the needs of the local community and employment potential available in the area.

6.2 Job Oriented Programmes Offered by the Community Colleges in India

- **Diplomas Offered by the Community Colleges**

(1) Computer System Technology
(2) Sales and Marketing Management
(3) Office Management and Secretaryship
(4) Cargo Management
(5) Printing Technology
(6) Computer Hardware Maintenance
(7) Hotel Management
(8) Air Conditioning and Refrigeration
(9) Beautician and Health Care
(10) Nursing Assistant and Nursing Midwifery
(11) Multipurpose Health Worker
(12) Home Nursing and Housekeeping
(13) Two Wheeler Mechanism
(14) Tailoring and Embroidery
(15) Small Business Development

(16) Automobile Service Maintenance (or) Four Wheeler Mechanism

(17) Electrical and Electronics

(18) Crop Plant Maintenance

(19) Pre-School Teacher Education

(20) Multipurpose Rural Development Worker (or) Multipurpose Social Worker

(21) Small Home Appliances Service and Repair

(22) Medial Lab Technology

(23) Medical Radiographic Assistant

(24) Sustainable Agriculture Worker

(25) Marine Engine Mechanism

(26) Clinical Nutrition

(27) Integrated Farm Development

(28) Diploma in Agrofarming

(29) Diploma in Motor Mechanic

(30) Computerized Financial Accounting

Certificate Courses offered by the Community Colleges

1. Driving and Automobile Maintenance
2. Play Ground Management
3. Wiring and Masonry
4. Masonry and Plumbing
5. Plumbing and Wiring

6.3 Nursing Assistant and Hotel Management - Outlines

1. Diploma In Nursing Assistant

Introduction

Nursing Assistant course is designed to train the female students of the community colleges in nursing skills. It is a great opportunity for the disadvantaged students to train in the community colleges at a low cost compared to the high fees charged by the private institutions. There is a great demand for Nursing Assistants both in the urban and in the rural areas and the students can easily get employed .The students can also work as a village health worker in her own village. The students are trained in Nursing procedures and Midwifery.

Objectives

- To provide the basic concept and principles of Nursing techniques and Nursing procedures.
- To provide basic knowledge to handle sterile instruments.
- To provide adequate knowledge on patient care.
- To provide first aid skills.
- To provide knowledge on mental health
- To provide knowledge on child health
- To provide adequate knowledge about the care during maternity cycle
- Antenatal Period
- Prenatal Period
- Postnatal Period
- To develop skills in
  - Unit cleaning and Bed making
  - Injection giving
  - Medicine giving
  - Temperature, Pulse and Respiration
  - Checking Blood Pressure
  - Dressing
- To provide adequate knowledge about maternity nursing
- To provide knowledge about basic medical care
- To provide knowledge about the nutritive value of food stuff
- To provide knowledge about hygiene, health and environmental sanitation

Job Opportunities

Field Jobs

- Nursing Assistant can be an instructor in health education.
- Nursing Assistant can be employed as a nursing assistant, health worker in hospitals, Clinics and village health centres.

Entry Qualification

(a) Education : 10th Passed and above
(b) Age : 15 years and above

Selection

Counselling - 30 hours of career Guidance from the experts

Contents of the Job Oriented Programme

PAPER I : Study of the Human Body – Micro Organisms Psychiatric and Disease

Unit	*Contents*	*Theory*	*Practical*
1.	Anatomy	→ Body as an Integrated whole → Types of bone → Erect and Moving Body → Bone Tissues → Structure of the Bone → Functions of the Bone	→ Unit Cleaning and Bed Making → Preparing aids for skeletal System
2.	Physiology	→ Types of muscles → Maintaining the Metabolism of the body → Functions of the Muscle → Integration and build of the Body.	→ Height and Weight Checking → Preparing Aids for muscular system.
3.	Various System of our body		→ Checking Blood Pressure
(a)	Circulatory System	→ Structure and Functions of the heart → Types of the blood cells → Functions of blood → Blood groups → Hemorrhage, Thrombosis	
(b)	Respiratory System	→ Structure and Function of the lungs → Define Respiration → Types of respiration → External heart compression	→ Checking Temperature Pulse and Respiration
(c)	Digestive System	→ Structure of the Abdomen → Functions of the Abdomen → Secretion of enzymes	→ Preparing Aids of digestive System
(d)	Excretory System	→ Structure of the kidney → Functions of the kidney → Fluid and electrolyte Balance	→ Urine Test → Reaction → Albumin, Sugar → Specific Gravity
(e)	Endocrine System	→ Thyroid, Para Thyroid → Adrenal, Islets of Langerhans → Pituitary glands (Anterior, Posterior)	
(f)	Reproductive System	→ Structure and functions of the Reproductive Organs	
(g)	Central Nervous System	→ Autonomic Nervous System → Sympathetic and Para → Sympathetic Nervous System → Sensory Nerve → Motor and Mixed Nerve → Structure and functions of the Brain	→ Changing the Position for the helpless patient → Mouth Care

Contd....

(h)	Sensory System	→ Structure and Function of the → Skin, Eye, Nose, Ear and Tongue	→ Eye, Ear, Nose Care
4.	Micro Biology	→ Introduction to Micro Organisms → Micro Organisms Present in Human body, soil environment → Sources, modes of infection → Pathogenic micro organisms → Identification, destruction of micro organisms Health worker's responsibilities	→ Preparing aids for modes of infection.
5.	Mental Health	→ Introduction → Define Mental health Psychiatry → Behaviour and basic therapies → Measures and facilities for prevention and early detection.	→ Giving Counselling
6.	Psychiatric Nursing	→ Early Detection of mental Disorder → Identifying mentalities Patient → Recognising problems of Adjustment in various life tages → Behaviour changes → Emergencies in Mental illness Aftercare and supervision	→ Rehabilitation Care
7.	Communicable Disease	→ Introduction → Immunity → Immunisation → Identifying communicable Diseases → Symptoms → Prevention → Control and Care	→ Collection of Specimens
8.	Communicable Diseases and Infection	→ Tuberculosis → AIDS → Cholera, Diarrhea → Typhoid Fever → Malaria, Poliomyelitis → Sexually Transmitted Disease → Venereal Disease	→ Local Application

PAPER II : Fundamental of Nursing

Unit	*Contents*	*Theory*	*Practical*
1.	Fundamental of Nursing	→ Definition of Nursing → Introduction to Nursing Concept → Health Organisation → Maintaining Health Environment	→ History Collection
2.	Nursing Services	→ Maintenance of Supplies and equipments → Another facilities → Maintenance of Records → Types of records → Types of reports	→ Post Operative bed
3.	Nursing Technique	→ Meeting Hygiene → Principles of Nursing → Comfort Measures → Comfort Needs	→ Injections (IM, IV, SC, ID)

4.	Nursing Procedures	→ Aseptic Practices → Surgical Asepsis → Medications and Therapies → Oral Medications → Local Applications → Injections	→ Dressing
5.	First Aid	→ Introduction to the first aid Definition of Promoting safety Consciousness → Inspires to bone joints → Wounds and hemorrhages → Poisons swallowed → Dog, Snake, Insect bites and Stings → Scald and Burns → Foreign bo dies in eye, ear, Nose and throat	→ Comfort Measures
6.	Emergency Nursing	→ Artificial Respiration → Approach to a Casualty → Handling & transport of Injured persons → Arrangement for the reception of a casualty in house.	→ Pediculosis Treatment → Bed Shampoo
7.	Specialty Nursing	Care of patient with → Respiratory System → Digestive System → Circulatory System → Urinary System → Nephrotic System → Neurotic System → ENT System	→ Giving Enema → Rectal Examination (Assisting)
8.	Basic Nursing	Care of Patient with → Preparative Care → Pre operative care → Post operative care	→ General Physical Examination (Assisting)

PAPER III : Maternal and Child Health

Unit	*Contents*	*Theory*	*Practical*
1.	Introduction to child Health	→ Growth and development of a child → Care of New born → Nutritional requirement of new Born → Agencies for child care and Welfare	
2.	Protection of Child health	→ Immunisation schedules → Abgor Score → General physical examination → Importance of breast feeding → Techniques of breast feeding → Adult education on child care	→ Preparing aids for immunisation Schedules
3.	Introduction to maternal Health	→ Care During Maternity cycle → Conception period → Antenatal Period → Prenatal Period → Postnatal Period → Organisation of maternal → Health care services	→ Perennial Care → Vaginal Douche
4.	Maternity Nursing	→ The reproductive System → Growth and Development of Foetus	→ Vaginal Examination (Assisting)

		→ Stages of labour → Frequency of labour → Normal labour → Complication of labour	
5.	Obstetrics Nursing	→ Obsessive Operators (Axis, Traction, Vacuum forceps) → High Risk for pregnancy → Abnormal labour → Abnormal purperium → Forms, Records and statistics → Training community health Worker	→ Rectal Suppositories
6.	Introduction to Community Health	→ Define community Health → Understanding the Community → Senior health services (FAO, WHO, UNICEF, CMAI)	
7.	Family Health	→ Environmental health & sanitation → Disposal of refuse → Domicilary health services → Definition for family planing → Methods (Permanent, Temporary)	→ Admission & Discharge

PAPER IV : Health and Hygiene

Unit	*Contents*	*Theory*	*Practical*
1.	Pharmacology	→ Definition of Pharmacology → Sources of Drugs → Preparation of drugs → Weight and measures → Abbreviation in common use → Action of drugs	→ Blood transfusion (Assisting)
2.	Basic Medicine	→ Introduction → Home Nursing & elementary → Medical care → Basic medical care → Drug legislation	→ Gastric Lavage
3.	Hygiene	→ Introduction to hygiene & Healthful living → Factor influences the poor Hygiene → Preventive measures → Mental hygiene & health	→ Sponge Bath
4.	Health	→ Physical Health → Periodical health examination → Health in home → Health in family, early → Children, adulthood and in Old age problems	→ Care of hair
5.	Nutrition	→ Introduction → Nutritive value of food stuff → The balanced Diet → Preparation & Preservation of Food → Vitamins (Fat, Water soluble) Malnutrition → Deficiency Diseases food → Adulteration practices → Nutrition education	→ Intravenous fluids (Assisting) → Naso gastric → Tube feeding

6.	Basic Sanitation and Environmental Sanitation	→ Basic Sanitation needs are village place towns and semi - urban areas → Disinfection → Sterilisation → Communicable Disease control → Sanitary and Health measures for special situations → Control, preventive care.	→ Use of flatus tube → Care of rubber hoods

Duration:

(a) *Diploma in Nursing Assistant*
21 Weeks X 30 Hrs per Week = 630 Hrs = 21 Credits

(b) *Internship and hands on Experience*
8 Weeks X 48Hrs per Week = 390 Hrs =13 Credits

Scheme and Format of Study

PAPER	Topics	Theory Hrs	Practicals Hrs	Total Hrs
A	Career Guidance and Counselling	30	-	30
B	Study of the Human Body -Micro organisms Psychiatric and Disease	60	90	150
C	Fundamentals of Nursing	60	90	150
D	Maternal and Child Health	60	90	150
E	Health and Hygiene	60	90	150
	Total	270	360	630

Internship and Hands on Experience

S.No	Programme	Duration	Hours	Credits
1	Hands on Experience/Internship	8 Weeks X 8 hrs per day	390 Hours	13 Credits
	Total	8 Weeks	390 Hours	13 Credits

Scheme of Evaluation:

Internals 50% 100 marks (40% Theory + 60% Practicals)
Externals* 50% 100 marks (40% Theory + 60% Practicals)
200 marks
*** To be conducted by NOS**

Eligibility Criteria:

A. Attendance 80%
B. Marks (Internal Assessment) 40%

Pass Criteria

a. 40% **Theory**
b. 40% **Practical**

List of Tools, Equipments and Materials

Equipments

1. Thermometer
2. Sphygmomanometer
3. Stethoscope
4. Cot with locker
5. Weighing Machine
6. Wheel Chair
7. Stretcher
8. Torch Light
9. Foetoscope
10. Protoscope
11. Opthalmoscope
12. Tonometer
13. Urinmometer
14. Valsellum Forceps
15. Arty Clamp (Curved & Straight)
16. Thumb Forceps
17. Cheatle Forceps
18. Vaginal Speculam
19. Sponge Holders
20. Back Rest
21. Cardiac Table
22. Bed Cradle
23. Oxygen Cylinder
24. Suction Apparatus
25. Tongue Depressor
26. Nasal Speculam
27. Tooth Extractor
28. Otoscope
29. Trolley
30. Tuning Fork
31. Spatula
32. Dissecting Forceps

33. Axis Traction Forceps
34. Vaccum Forceps
35. Focus Light
36. IV Stand
37. Enema can with tube
38. Intravenous fluids (DNS, RL, NS, 5%Dex, 10%Dex, 25%Dex)

Tools

1. Basin
2. Duster
3. Broom
4. Mattress
5. Brush (Nail)
6. Linen
7. Draw Sheet
8. Rubber Sheet
9. Pillow
10. Bucket
11. Kidney tray
12. Bed pan
13. Cleaning powder
14. Gauze
15. Cotton
16. Pad
17. Bandage
18. Drum
19. Measurement Jar
20. Syringes with Needle
21. Sputum cup
22. Plaster
23. Specimen bottle
24. IV set
25. Blood set

26. Apron
27. Mask
28. Gloves
29. Gown
30. Jug
31. Mug or Dipper
32. Towel
33. Swab Sticks
34. Cotton Rings
35. Air Cushion
36. Restrains
37. Tape measure
38. Bowel
39. Basket
40. Sprit Lamp
41. Charts (TPR Chart, Admission & Discharge Chart)
42. Scissors

Solutions

1. Savlon
2. Dettol
3. Hydrogen Peroxide
4. Betadine
5. I.G. (Ithmol Glycerine)
6. Boric Acid
7. Glycerine
8. Vaseline
9. Benedict Solution
10. Tincture Benzoine
11. Blue, Red litmus paper
12. Sprit
13. Potassium permanganate $kmno_4$
14. Carbolic lotion
15. Liquid Paraffin
16. Gentian Violet

Audio Visual Aids

1. Respiratory System
2. Circulatory System
3. Reproductive System
4. Urinary System
5. Central Nervous System
6. Muscular System
7. Skeletal System
8. Anatomical bones

Suggested Reference Books

S. No	*Name of the Book*	*Name of the Author*
1.	The text book for the health worker (Volume I)	A.M. Chacklay
2.	The text book for the health worker (Volume II)	A. M. Chacklay
3.	The principles and practice of Nursing (Volume I	Sr. Nancy
4.	The principles and practice of Nursing (Volume II)	Sr. Nancy
5.	Principles of Nutrition and Dietetics	Dr. M. Swaminathan
6.	Myles text Book for Midwives 12th edition	Linder K. Brown and V. Rath Bennett
7.	The text book of Microbiology IV edition	C. K. Jeyaram Panikar, R. Ananthanarayanan.
8.	Parks Text Book of preventive and social Medicine IV edition	K. Park
9.	A community Health nursing manual	Mrs. R. K. Sood
10.	Essentials of community health nursing II edition	J.E. Part, K. Park
11.	Best of Health	Edison samraj
12.	Plants that heal	Dr. J.C. Kurian

2. Diploma in Hotel Management

Introduction

Hotel Management course is designed to train the students of the community colleges in Front Office, Housekeeping, Food and Service and Administration skills. Community Colleges provides a great opportunity for the disadvantaged students to pursue a career in Hotel Management with affordable fees. On completion of the course the students get employed. The hotel industry has grown rapidly and there is a constant demand for Hotel Management students. The students of community colleges are always a step ahead of other students due to their life coping skills.

Objectives:

1. To prepare skilled human resource for the hotel and catering industry keeping in view the future projection of the requirement.
2. To impart thorough knowledge and develop technical skills in various aspects of food production and service.
3. To develop personality traits like confidence, good etiquette, effective communication, pleasing personality, salesmanship and above all a willingness to serve.
4. To develop cost consciousness for maximum utilization of time, energy and resources and an eye for detail.
5. To develop work ethics and adequate work habits essential for working in a team.
6. To acquaint the student with the employment potential in the Hospitality Industry.

Job Opportunities

Field Job:

1. Front Office Assistants in Three star and Five star Hotels.
2. House keeping Assistants / Supervisors
3. Food and Beverage Assistants / Supervisors
4. Bell Captain
5. Travel Desk

Entry Qualification

10th pass and above
15 years and above

Selection

Counselling - 30 hours of career Guidance from the experts.

Contents of the Job Oriented Programme

PAPER I : Introduction to the Hotel Industry

Unit	Content	Theory
1.	Importance of Tourism	Importance of Tourism - Market Share in Global Tourism - Domestic Tourism
2.	Hotel Industry	Introduction - Definition - Origin
3.	International Airlines	Role of an International Airlines in the Tourism Industry - Air Fares

4.	Travel Agent	Role of a Travel Agent - Role Chart - Duties and responsibilities of a Travel Agent
5.	Transport Systems	Introduction to Transports Systems in India
6.	Types of Hotels	Categorization based on Factors - Categorization by Locations - Categorization by number - Categorization by type of clientele- Categorisation by length of Guest stay.
7.	Facilities offered by Star Hotels	Classification of Star Hotels - Procedure of Classification as per the facilities offered to the Customers.
8.	Principles and function of Hotel Management	Division of Work - Authority - Organising - Unitary Control - Unitary Direction- Establishment Goals
9.	Line of Organisation	Line Organisati on - Staff Organisation - Line and Staff Organisation
10.	Qualities of a Leader	Qualities of a Leader- Types of Leader
11.	Management of Resources	Management of Resources -Money - Space - Material - Food Materials - Cleaning Materials - Equipment - Staff - Time - Energy
12.	Communication	Types of Communication - Characteristics of a good Communication - Process of Communication - Methods of Communication - Barriers to Communication
13	Importance of Catering and Forecasting Future Trends	Importance of Catering and Forecasting Future Trends - Minimizing costs still maintaining quality
14.	Front Office	Definition of Front Office - front Office as Sources of Information
15.	Qualities of Front Office	Qualities of Front Office - Salesman - Problem Solvers - A reference Point - Coordinators - Image Builders - Essential Attributes - Front Office Organisational Hierarchy.
16.	Front Office Salesmanship -	Knowledge of Products - Room - Restaurant and Bars - Arcade - Supporting Services - City Information - Sa les Promotion - Guests Needs - Desire to Help - Communication
17	Importance of Hygiene and Sanitation	Hygiene - Sanitation - Safety Standards - Methods of maintaining - Hygiene standards - Effective Sanitation - Safety Consciousness- Standards
18	The Ro le of Telephone Exchange	Various Registers in use in the Exchange - Log Book - Complaint Register - Handing over Register.
19.	Duties and Responsibilities of Telephone Operation	Qualities of a Good Telephone operator - Punctuality - Personal Hygiene - Acc uracy - Speed - Co -operation - Clarity of Speech - A sense of Responsibility on the Job - Secrecy - Memory Concentration - Application and Quickness
20	Handling of Equipment	Handling of Equipment - Maintenance Equipment - Procedures to be adopted for falure of equipment.

PAPER II : Front Office Administration

Unit	Content	Theory
1.	Importance of Job Description	Importance of Job Description - Job Description of Front Office Assistants - Job Position - Category - Reports to - Job Definition - Direct Control - assigned area of activity - Departments that Front Office - Coordinates - Room Report
2.	Arrivals and Departure Procedures for Guest and VIP	Special Arrangement for groups and VIPs - VIP Amenities Voucher Copy
3.	Front Office Procedures for Emergencies	Lost and Found Procedures - Fire Handling Procedures - Guest's Death - Precautions to avoid thefts.
4.	Functions of Information Department	Maintain Guest Portfolio - Alphabetical Index - Receive Messages - Handling Incoming Messages Format - Control Guest Room Keys - Handle Guest Mail- Insured Mail
5.	Providing Information to Guests	Aids used for the Task of Providing Information
6.	Modes of Reservation Requests	Modes of Reservation Requests - Types of Rooms - Group Reservation - Arrival Procedures

7.	Rights and Liabilities of Hotels and Travel Agencies	Rights and Liabilities of Hotels and Travel Agencies in Room Reservation - Discounts and Allowances - Commission Terms.
8.	Hotel Tariff Terms	Reservation Terms - Cancellation Terms FITS - Group Cancellation - Terms for Payment of Hotel Bills.
9.	Procedure for Registration of Guest	Registers - Registration Cards - Advantages - Night Clerk's Report
10.	Job Description of Front Office Cashier	Cashier - Job Description - Category - Assigned area of Activity - Hours of Operation - Authority
11.	Foreign Currency	Meaning - Procedure for Accepting Foreign Exchange - Procedure for Processing Foreign Currency - Procedure for Handling Credit Cards.
12.	Guest Folio	Meaning - Formats - City ledger - Payments from Company Employees
13.	Processing Crew Allowances Vouchers	Procedure to process - Making payments of Petty Cash amount on behalf of Guest
14.	Safety Locker Management	Procedure when a guest desires to keep any Valuables in safety.
15.	Job Description of Night Auditor	Job position - Category - Responsible to - Directly Controls - Supervision - Assigned Area of Activity
16.	Transcript	Meaning - Definition - Procedure for making a Transcript.
17.	Lobby	Meaning of Lobby - Importance of Lobby - Departmental Hierarchy
18.	Bell Captain	Job Description of a Bell Captain - Reports to - Directly Controls - Assigned area of Activity
19.	Left Luggage Procedure	Meaning - Receipt - Delivery - Scanty Baggage - Wake up call procedure.
20.	Lobby Staff	Duties of Lobby Staff - Departments Coordinating with the Lobby

PAPER III : Housekeeping

Unit	Content	Theory
1.	Introduction to Housekeeping	Meaning Definition
2.	Layout of the Housekeeping Department	Floor Pantries Meaning - Maintenance of Floor Pantries
3.	Hierarchy of Housekeeping Department	Job Description of Housekeeping Personnel.
4.	Housekeeping Co ordination	- Co-ordination - Recruitment and Selection Procedures
5.	Qualities of Housekeeping Staff	Briefing and Scheduling of Staff
6.	VIP's in the House	Policies and Procedures for VIP's in the House - Knowledge of different types of Rooms.
7.	Content of the Maids Cart	Procedure for Cleaning the Room and Making a Bed - Preparing a Room Report
8.	Role of the Control Desk	Co-ordination with the Front Of fice - Engineering Department - Types of Registers and Files Maintained
9.	Housekeeping Equipment's	Description of Housekeeping Equipment's - Procedures for requesting Fresh Linen - Guest Supplies - Cleaning Supplies
10.	Maintenance	Records - Floor Linen Room - Public Area - Shopping Arcade - Store Room - Swimming Pools
11.	Practices and Procedures	Linen Room - Storage Conditions - Storage Tips - Types of Linen used.
12.	Par Stock	Par Stock - Definition - Importance - How to establish Par Stock
13.	Inventory Control	Stock Taking - Methods and Principles Involved.
14.	Budgeting	Types of Budget - How to make a Budget - Capital Budget - Operational Budget

15.	Lost and Found Procedure	Meaning & Procedure
16	Cleaning Methods	Cleaning Methods - Various Factors - General Principles - Basic Methods - Carpet upholstery - Cleaning Agents - General Principles
17.	Laundry Services	Valet Service - Soil Removal - Bleaching - Floral Art - Pest Control
18.	Fire Prevention	Types of Extinguishers - Methods of Fire control
19.	First Aid	First Aid - Importance - Material required - Procedures
20.	Housekeeping Training	Orientation - Importance of Training - Training Tips

PAPER IV : Food and Service Management

Unit	Content	Theory
1.	Organisation of Kitchen Spaces	Layout of Kitchens - Maintenance of Kitchens - Simple Layout Plans
2.	Different Type of Kitchens	Different Type of Kitchens - combination of Spaces - Work Area - Movement at Work
3.	Storage Spaces	Basic Factor - Location of Storage Spaces - Types of Storage - Planning Storage Spaces
4.	Service Area	Location - Structural Designing - Planning Service Area - Smooth Flow of Work - Space Utilisation - Prompt Service.
5.	Classification of Equipment	Weight of Equipment - Size of Equipment - Order of Use - Mode of operation
6.	Selection of Equipment	Basic Factors - Size and Type of Establishment - Menu - Utility of Design - Price - Sources of Supply
7.	Purchasing Equipment	Purchase Procedure - Purchasing Methods - Purchasing Decisions - Factors Determined - Payment of Equipment
8.	Care and Maintenance of Equipment	Schedule for Maintenance - Cooking Equipment - Hot Plates - Gas Stoves and Ranges - Ovens - Refrigerators - Preparation Equipment - Maintenance Cost
9.	Characteristics of Food	Types of Foods - Natural Fo ods - Processed Foods - Importance of Quality - Quantitative aspects of Quality
10.	Food Purchasing	Food Purchasing - Food Buyer - Purchasing Activity - Functions of a Food Buyer - Buying Food - Formal Buying
11.	Receiving and Storage of Food	Receiving - Delivery Methods - General Procedure for Storage - Store Keeping - Maintenance of Food Quality in Storage
12.	Menu Planning	Menu Planning - Functions - Reasons for Planning Menus - The Situation - The Customer - Drafting Menus - Menu Display
13.	Food Production System	Convenience - Food Production Process - Cooking Methods on the Nutritional Quality of Foods - Methods of Holding Food.
14.	Food Service	Styles of Service - Methods of Waiter Service - Presentation and Display of Food
15.	Dishwashing	Detergents - Action of Detergents - Abrasives - The Dishwashing Process - Pot or Pan washing
16.	Hygiene and Sanitation	Environmental Hygiene and Sanitation - Site - Structure Equipment - Furniture - Fittings - Ventilation - Lighting - Water - Supply - Waste Disposal
17.	Safety	Safety Standards - Accidents from Structural inadequacies - Accidents from improper placement of Equipment in Spaces - Safety Taining
18	Labour Laws	Laws affecting food service establishment.
19.	Food Laws	Food standards in India
20.	Consumer Education	Awareness

PAPER V : Personnel and Catering Management

Unit	Content	Theory
1.	Importance of Personnel Management	Organisational objectives

2.	Personnel Policies	Effective Utilisation of Human Resource- Establishment of Healthy Wor king Relationships - Encouragement of maximum development of individuals
3.	Planning	Definition of Planning- Organizational Planning
4.	Types of Plans	Advantages of Planning
5.	Staffing Needs	Matching skills for job requirements
6.	Conditions of Employment	Terms and Conditions of Employment - Personnel Administration
7.	Recruitment Procedures	Recruitment Procedure - Sources of Recruitment
8.	Staff Welfare	Staff Welfare - Promotion Needs -
9.	Understanding Physical Needs and Physiological Needs	Maslow's Hierarchy of Needs
10.	The Need for Training and Development	Training Programmes - Areas of Training - Development - Process of Development
11.	Financial Management	Definition of Financial Management- Financial Accounting
12.	Cost Control	Components of Costs - Behavior of Costs - Concept of Contribution and Break - Even
13.	Food Cost Control	Methods of Controlling Food Costs
14.	Factors Responsible for loss	Calculations and Cost Statements
15.	Pricing Structure	Methods of Pricing
16.	Factors affecting Pricing	Factors affecting Pricing - Making Pricing Decisions
17.	To study the Purchasing Power of the Customers	Purchasing Power as Related to the Expectations of Customers - Environmental Conditions
18.	Principles of Accounting	Golden Rules of Accounting - Petty Cash Book
19.	Accounting concepts	Book Keeping
20.	Ledger	Ledger Posting - Balance Sheet

Duration

(A) Diploma in Hotel Management
21 Weeks X 30 Hrs per Week = 630 Hrs = 21 Credits

(B) Internship and hands on Experience
8 Weeks X 48Hrs per Week = 390 Hrs =13 Credits

Scheme and Format of Study

PAPER	Topics	Theory	Practical	Hours
	Career Guidance and Counselling	30	-	30
I	Introduction to Hotel Industry	48	72	120
II	Front Office Administration	48	72	120
III	Hotel House keeping	48	72	120
IV	Food and Service Management	48	72	120
V	Personnel and Financial Management	48	72	120
	Total	**270**	**360**	**630**

Internship and Hands on Experience

S.No	Programme	Duration	Hours	Credits
1.	Hands on Experience/Internship	8 Weeks X 8 hrs per day	390 Hours	13 Credits
	Total	**8 Weeks**	**390 Hours**	**13 Credits**

Scheme of Evaluation:

Internals	50%	100 marks (40% Theory + 60% Practicals)
Externals*	50%	100 marks (40% Theory + 60 Practicals)
		200 marks

* To be conducted by NOS

Eligibility Criteria

(A) Attendance 80%

(B) Marks (Internal Assessment) 40%

Pass Criteria

(a) 40% Theory

(b) 40% Practical

Infrastructure

1. Kitchen (for 20 students)
2. Baking equipments.
3. Model service room sufficiently furnished.
4. Computer and Accountancy records for Front Office
5. Model Room for Housekeeping.

Books for Reference:

S. No	*Name of the Book*	*Name of the Author*
1.	Hotel Front Office Training Manual	Sudhir Andrews
2.	Hotel Housekeeping Training Manual	Sudhir Andrews
3.	Food and Beverage Service Training Manual	Sudhir Andrews
4.	Modern Cookery Vol.	Thangam E. Philip
5.	Careers in Hotel Management	Mamta Agarwal and Arun Agarwal
6.	Theory of Catering	Kinton and Cessarani

7

Evaluation and Assessment of Skills

7.1 Evaluation and Assessment of Skills

The Evaluation and Assessment of the Skills of the incumbents of the Community College at present is completely *internal* and done by the Community College with the help of technical and field experts. The evaluation is aimed at the testing of the skills rather than the absorption of information. The evaluation is jointly done by the Life Skill Instructor, Work Skills Instructor, Industrial Supervisor supplemented by the self-assessment of the student of the Community College, thus making the evaluation comprehensive and purposeful, determining the attainment of skills.

The knowledge and skills component should be given equal weightage. This evaluation is to be continuous, transparent and should contain checks and balances within the system to ensure credibility.

The Diploma or the certificate is signed by the Director of the college as well as the Industrial Partner who has trained the students in the particular fields of specialisation.

7.2 Scheme of Evaluation of Life Skills and Work Skills Programme in the Community Colleges

I. LIFE SKILLS

1. Life Coping Skills

1.	Assignments	4x5 = 20 marks
2.	Two Tests	2x5 = 10 marks

3.	Oral Presentation	10 marks
4.	Group Discussion	10 marks
5.	Poster Presentation	10 marks
6.	Final Examination	40 marks
	Total	**100 marks**

2. Interpersonal Relations and Communication Skills

1.	Two Assignments	10x5 = 50 marks
2.	Two Tests	5x2 = 10 marks
3.	Group Discussion	10 marks
4.	Public Speaking	10 marks
5.	Just a Minute	10 marks
6.	Final Examination	40 marks
	Total	**100 marks**

3. Developmental English

1.	Ten Letters and Ten Paragraphs Writing	10 marks
2.	20 Exercises (News Paper Clippings)	10 marks
3.	20 Categories (Flowers, towns etc)	10 marks
4.	200 words from the dictionary	10 marks
5.	Two Tests	20 marks
6.	Final Examination	40 marks
	Total	**100 marks**

4. Basic Computer Applications

1. Theory – 80 Marks

1.	Assignment	10 marks
2.	Seminar	10 marks
3.	Six Tests	6x5 = 30 marks
4.	Final Examination	40 marks
	Total	**100 marks**

2. Practical – 120 Marks

1.	Six Tests	6x10 = 60 marks
2.	Final Examination	40 marks
	Total	**100 marks**

II. WORK SKILLS

Each Paper will be evaluated for 200 Marks	
Internal Assessment	100 marks
Final Assessment	100 marks
Total	**200 marks**

Internal Assessment

1.	Two Written Tests	2x10 = 20 marks
2.	Two Oral Presentations	2x10 = 20 marks
3.	Two Group Discussions	2x10 = 20 marks
4.	Two Assignments	2x10 = 20 marks
5.	Two Quizzes or Objective Tests or Two Practical Tests or Two Field Visits	2x10 = 20 marks
	Total	**100 marks**

Final Assessment

1.	Theory Three Hour Examination	40 marks
2.	Practical Three Hour Test Examination	60 marks
	Total	**100 marks**

8
Internship and Hands on Experience

8.1 Internship and Hands on Experience

Every Community College tries its best to find places for internship for all its students in collaboration with the Industrial Partners. The common experience has been that most of the students who have done well in the internship have found a placement in the same institution where they went for Training and Hands on Experience. It is highly recommended that every Community College has a placement officer who co-ordinates with the Industrial Partner for internship. It is also imperative that the staff members of the Community College visit the student on site and obtain the assessment of the Industrial Supervisor. The Evaluation and Assessment of Skills is done by four people: Life Skills Instructor, Work Skills Instructor, Industrial Supervisor and Self Assessment of the Individual Student. To facilitate this Assessment, the MCRDCE has evolved a Skill Assessment Chart that is filled in by all the above four people. The sample of such a Skill Chart is given below.

8.2 Evaluation of the Community College Students

Skills Assessment Chart

Name : ______________________

Job Oriented Programme : ______________________

Place of Training : ______________________

Campus Admitted : ______________________

Please Rate the following skills by a Tick Mark

5 – Excellent; 4 – Very Good; 3 – Above Average; 2 – Average and 1 – Poor.

A

S. No	Personal Skills	5	4	3	2	1
1.	Punctuality					
2.	Sincerity					
3.	Self-Esteem					
4.	Responsibility					
5.	Reliability					
6.	Spontaneity					
7.	Problem Solving					
8.	Presence of Mind					
9.	Hard Working					
10.	Stress Management					

B

	Social Skills	5	4	3	2	1
1.	Listening					
2.	Patience					
3.	Hospitality					
4.	Overcoming Shyness					
5.	Accepting ones own faults					

C

	Communication Skills	5	4	3	2	1
1.	Dialogue					
2.	Oral and Written					
3.	Presentation Skills					
4.	Good Expression					
5.	Ability to understand					

D

	Language Skills	5	4	3	2	1
1.	Multilingual					
2.	Speaking					
3.	Writing					

E

	Creative Skills	5	4	3	2	1
1.	Updating of Skills					
2.	Innovative					
3.	Risk Taking					
4.	Imaginative					
5.	Industrious					
6.	Other Talents (Singing, Dancing etc)					

F

	Leadership Skills	5	4	3	2	1
1.	Empathy					
2.	Impartiality					

3.	Co-ordination					
4.	Animation					
5.	Team Building					
6.	Approachability					
7.	Dynamic					
8.	Resourcefulness					
9.	Initiative					
10.	Organisation Skils					

8.3 Evaluation of the Community College Students Skills Assessment Chart

G Work Skills Programme

Please Rate the following skills by a Tick Mark:
5 – Excellent; 4 – Very Good; 3 – Above Average; 2 – Average; 1 – Poor

S. No	Work Skills	5	4	3	2	1
1.	Resistor Colour code Identification					
2.	Resistor Checking					
3.	Capacitor					
4.	Diode					
5.	Transistor					
6.	Transformer					
7.	SMPS Circuit Tracking					
8.	SMPS Fault Rectification Tracking					
9.	Monitor Circuit Tracking					
10.	Monitor Fault Rectification					
11.	Pentium Board Checking					
12.	Floppy Disk Drive Fault Rectification					
13.	Keyboard Fault Rectification					
14.	Hard Disk Drive Fault Rectification					
15.	CD Drive Installation					
16.	Driver Fault Installation					
17.	Diagnostic Software Packages					
18.	Virus Scanning					
19.	Assembling					
20.	Trouble Shooting					

Signature:

Industrial Supervisor / Work Skill Instructor / Life Skill Instructor

	Summary	Max	Results
A	Personal Skills	50	
B	Social Skills	25	
C	Communication Skills	25	
D	Language Skills	15	
E	Creative Skills	30	
F	Leadership Skills	50	
G	Work Skills	100	
	TOTAL	295	

Result : ________________

9
Preparation for Employment

9.1 Preparation for Employment

Part I – Getting Ready:

Job Application is the first contact that the candidate makes with the Employer. If the job application is ✔ the beginning is good. The proverb says, "A job well begun, is half done".

Application has two parts:

- Application
- Personal Details

Application: Please ensure that the following details are incorporated in the application.

- Your name and address
- Company's name and address
- Date of Application
- Subject (Post applied for)
- Reference
- Salutation
- Text
- Closing
- Courtesy Yours truly/Yours sincerely (not yours obediently etc.)
- Signature
- Enclosure

Check, Check, Check and Check.......

- As if Checking with a magnifying glass... carefully, patiently, looking for any mistakes.... Aiming perfection in the application.

(Please prepare two or three models of good application and have this understood by the students. Please tell them that they need to do the necessary modification, as required from case to case.)

Personal Details:

Different names, but means the same: Bio Data; Curriculum Vitae (CV); Resume.

Bio Data will contain these details : Name, Address, Phone Number (if available), Age and Date of Birth, Academic Qualification, Technical Qualification, Vocational Training, Internship (Apprenticeship), Extra Curricular Activities (Arts, Literature, Sports), wherever asked for height and weight, for higher jobs: Career / Life Objective, Experience, Strengths*, References, Date of Bio Data, Signature.

In the application the student will be giving details of strengths only. However, she/he will be prepared to state a few weaknesses in the interview. The boss may ask: "You have given details of your strengths. Don't you have any weaknesses? Are you perfect?" We must coach the students to answer this question. The answer should be such that the weakness itself may appear to be strength. Example: My weakness is impatience. When I see a job not done on time, I get impatient. Another example: My weakness is that I get angry very quickly when I see someone not being tolerant. Let the answer be genuine and also look genuine. A "smart" answer thinking that the boss is a fool will not help the student.

(Please prepare few model bio data and let the students learn to prepare their own bio data. It has to be genuine, authentic and her/his own.)

Quality of Application: Tell the students the importance of quality of application. Application is the first contact with the Employer. The first impression is the best impression. Therefore, if the job application is good the student has made the right beginning.

Quality of Application: Paper used; Handwritten or typewritten – when; Typing Quality; Enclosures – quality; quality of photograph – recently taken; envelope used for sending the application.

Mailing and Quality of mailing: Ordinary post; Registered Post – if asked for. Courier – yes, good courier; inland letter – no, unless specified so; post card – no, unless specified so;

Enclosures: What to enclose? Certificates – no to originals. Photo copies of certificates – if asked for. Photograph, only if asked for. Go by the direction/instructions given in the advertisement.

Envelope: Good envelope; Long and broad envelope; How many times do you fold; affixing stamp/pasting; To address (Receiver's address); From address (Sender's address); super scribe (writing the job code number on the top left corner of the envelope)

Check, check, check....before posting the envelope

Part II – Looking for Opportunities

Avenues: Employment Exchange; Employment News; Daily papers like The Hindu, The Times of India, The Daily Thanthi, Eenadu, etc., Private Employment Agencies, Local Times (like in Chennai Adayar Times etc.)

Employment Exchange: Why go by what people say? Why go by the past? Sometimes it works. Don't lose an opportunity by neglect. Don't lose an opportunity by perceptions. Register – Renew (periodically) – Revise (if you have acquired a new qualification or experience)

Advertisements: Regularly look for....on a daily basis. All papers, if possible; Do not neglect small companies; Do not neglect small positions; You need a foothold. (Paper - Buy (?), Collectively buy, borrow OR go to reading rooms).

Local Times: Example – Adayar Times, Mylapore Times etc., in Chennai. Get them free.

Private Employment Agencies: Don't part with too much money. Don't pay for overseas job. Look for only local jobs.

Periodically check with the agencies. (Overseas jobs: Make inquiries about the agency, thoroughly check. Only if you are convinced about the agency, deal with them. Be careful that you are not cheated).

Other avenues: Institutional Notice Boards; TV advertisements; Web sites (example: www.naukri.com)

Unsolicited: 1. Applications to companies. 2. Walk in requests

Unsolicited: (Sources and How)
Advertisement – refer to their success
Press news, annual reports, Employment advertisements – Yellow Pages, Near your home place.
Explore, explore, explore, explore...............

Walk in requests:

- Polite, courteous
- Hesitate to leave, but don't be a pest
- Ask, "When can I come to check again".
- Drop in occasionally. Say you thought business had improved .. expansion etc., However, don't be a nuisance by very frequent visits. Periodic, but not very frequent.
- Can you suggest some other place?
- After few visits: "Can you recommend to someone else who may need?"
- After you have known them little more, "Can I use your name as reference?"
- Give them feedback if they have referred you to a person or suggested a place.
- Be extra polite and courteous every time. But don't overdo.
- Keep your esteem. Don't fall at the feet of people.
- Give them regular feed back. How you are progressing. What jobs did you apply for. What interviews you went. What have you learnt of late. What new skills you have learnt. If you have added anything to your Portfolio book, show them. What efforts you are making etc., Let them feel that you have confidence in them.

Useful Tips:

- Learn every day something. No day should pass without your having learnt something new.
- Keep a pocket note book and pen – and carry always ... wherever you go.
- Keep telling as many people as you can of your efforts to get a job
- Don't listen to the pessimists
- You need a foot hold, take any job that comes along
- There is no job menial. Believe in dignity of labour.

Be Swift, Be Steady

Combine the qualities of the hare and the tortoise

Part III - Preparing for the Interview:

Days Ahead: Keep papers ready. Keep Address ready. Keep your dresses ready. Keep the documents ready. Keep Portfolio book ready. Keep copy of application ready. Keep copy of the advertisement ready. Keep photocopies of the certificates ready. Keep photocopy of the interview call letter at home.

Prepare a floppy if possible and store: (a) a word document (b) Power Point (c) copy of your application.

Brush up subjects. Imagine possible questions and prepare answers. Rehearse, rehearse, and rehearse. Relax • Meditate • Visualise.

See the place of interview in advance, if possible. It will be easy for you to go to the place on the day of interview.

What to carry: Copy of the application; copy of the advertisement; interview call letter in original; photo copies of certificates; originals of the certificates; Portfolio book; Floppy; Pocket note book; Pen, pencil; Calculator (if you have); Writing pad; A book to read (light reading material); Adequate cash; Water; Few biscuits; Few sheets of paper; Proper folder or file to carry the certificates and documents. Keep them in a proper order so that when asked for you can take them out without wasting time or looking clumsy.

On the day: Go early. • If need be, go to toilet and be at ease. * Inform that you have come. • Sit down, relax and read, if you prefer. • Be visible. • Be calm. Show you are calm.

During the Interview:

- Sit relaxed
- Listen, listen, listen.
- Be quick, but don't rush through with the answers like a bullet express. Give sufficient pauses where required
- Write and show
- Use graphics, use the learning techniques in appropriate way
- Be confident, slow and assertive
- If you find a PC on the table of the interviewer, at the right time, suggest to him/her to have a look at the Power point presentation you have in the floppy. Or the word document, whatever is useful for the moment.
- Use hook technique. Throw seeds of questions for which you are well prepared with the answers.

Ongoingly:

• Learn, learn, learn • Be the ready maid – well prepared and poised • Continuous improvement • No day passes without your having improved in some way or other - without having learnt something new.

Think Success, Dream Success, Breathe Success

Model Application for Employment

From:

A. K. Meena
No. 11, Patel Nagar 3rd Street,
Adayar,
CHENNAI - 600 020

To:

The Personnel Manager,
Ashok Leyland,
35, N.S.C. Bose Road,
CHENNAI - 600 001

Sir,

Sub: *Application for the position of Office Assistant*

Ref: Your advertisement in *"The Hindu"* dated 05.01.2006

With reference to your advertisement as above, I have pleasure in submitting my application for the post of Office Assistant in your esteemed concern.

You will find from the enclosed Bio Data that I have all the requisite qualifications necessary for the position advertised for.

I am enthusiastic and eager to be an employee of your reputed organization.

I assure you that I will be an asset to the organization and will contribute best through hard and sincere work.

Looking forward to hear from you.

With sincere thanks,

Yours truly,

Signature.................
A. K. Meena

January 5, 2006
Encl: Bio Data
(You can also use "Yours sincerely," in the place of "Yours Truly")

Sample of an unsolicited application for employment

From:

A. K. Meena
No. 11, Patel Nagar 3rd Street,
Adayar,
Chennai - 600 020

To:

The Personnel Manager,
Ashok Leyland,
35, N.S.C. Bose Road,
Chennai - 600 001

Sir,

Sub: Application for the position of Office Assistant

It has been my dream for long that I should associate with a reputed concern like yours. Inspired by such a dream, I have pleasure in submitting my candidature for the position of Office Assistant or a suitable position in your esteemed organization.

A detailed bio data is enclosed for your kind perusal.

I am enthusiastic and eager to be an employee of your reputed organization.

I assure you that I will be an asset to the organization and will contribute best through hard and sincere work.

Looking forward to hear from you.

With sincere thanks,

Yours truly,

Signature................
A.K. Meena

January 5, 2006

Bio Data

Name	:	**A. K. Meena**
Address	:	11-C, Nehru Nagar, 3rd Street, Adayar, Chennai 600 020
Contact Telephone	:	24422101 (pp)
Age	:	21
Date of Birth	:	4.08.1984
Height	:	162 cms
Weight	:	59 kgs
Qualification	:	**Educational**
1.		Passed Higher Secondary School Examination. (12th Standard) with 58% marks
2.		Passed 12 months "Community

	College" programme, specialising in Office Assistant.
	Technical
1.	Passed Typewriting - Higher (English)
2.	Certificate programme in Computer Applications from ABCD Technical Institute
Vocational Training	6 months training in Office Assistant as part of Community College programme. I have been trained in Computing Skills, Handling Xerox, Fax, Business Correspondence, Drafting, Typing...etc.
Internship	2 months of intensive training in the Flower Pvt. Ltd., at Chennai. this period, I had the opportunity to handle Xerox Machine, Fax, Computer and work along with the regular staff of that Company.
Extra Curricular	1. Active member of the Social Service League of the School. As part of SSL, I have worked in various camps 2. Won prizes for Tamil oratory competition 3. Member of School Foot ball team
My strengths	: • Hard working • Sincere • Willingness to learn • Honest • Sharp in mathematics • Good handwriting • Robust health • Can withstand long hours of work • Good at design • Excellent knowledge of nursing • Good speed on the pc keyboard

Experience	:	Worked as Lab attendant with Vedic Laboratories for 6 months
References	1.	Mr. Abcde Efghi Secretary, Vedic Pvt. Ltd, No. 56, Spiritual Street, Adayar, Chennai, 600 020
	2.	Ms Jklmn Nopqr Coordinator, Community College, xxxpet Chennai, 600 018
Additional skills	:	Possess Driving Licence Possesses valid Passport.

(Signature)

Date :

10

Industrial Community Partnership

10.1 Industrial Collaboration

The Community College cannot succeed without the active participation and collaboration of the industrial, rural, agricultural, commercial and service organisations of the locality. The above sectors come to assist the Community College in the following five ways.

(1) Designing the curriculum for various job oriented courses.

(2) Serving as members of the advisory board.

(3) Being part time instructors for teaching and assessment in the College.

(4) On the job training for the students in the work place.

(5) Job placement for students who have been trained in the Community Colleges.

- Memorandum of Understanding could be signed with the industries for all the above five areas of collaboration.
- A few representatives form the above sectors industrial, commerce and service sectors could also serve as the members of the governing body of the College.

10.2 Industrial Collaboration and Community Colleges – A Key to Employability

Introduction:

Community College is a college with a difference. The difference lies in the way the formation is imparted to the excluded only. This difference in the college is presented to the Public, Academicians, NGOs, Management Professional Bank Officials, Commercial and Business Sectors and Industrial Partners and Executives at different dates and in different ways.

This introduction facilitated them to understand better the *"Need Analysis"* and then they realised the importance of such college as *Alternative System* to the *Existing System of Education.* It is this alternative system that makes the excluded (the school drop-outs, the early school leavers, and the drop-outs from various other educational institutions) to match education with employment.

Expectation of Industry

Employers today are interested in well-informed graduates or professionals. They are in need of skilled persons who are integrated and who have more common sense and practical mind-set to do a job. They are also looking for candidates with total involvement, greater enthusiasm, better commitment and desire to persevere and to learn more and more.

Measures To Meet Their Expectations

1. Clear presentation of the Concept of Community College to the Industrialists.
2. Representing the same concept to Industrial Trainers / Supervisors in the presence of their bosses.
3. Involving them in the formulation of syllabus and assessment of students' performance.
4. Regular visit and contacts with them.
5. Association of the Industrial Trainers in teaching the subjects.
6. At specified intervals, visit to industries with students during internship.
7. Sending the excluded to Field Placement according to the learning speed and according to the three-tier assessment.
8. Follow up of the candidate at every phase of the training-on campus, outside the campus, in-house training and in other places.

9. Memorandum Of Understanding (MOU) or Letter of exchange can be obtained from Industrialists, depending upon the association of the College, the Quality of Training and their involvement.
10. Openness to change the procedure and classes as per the advice of the partners and in accordance with the advancement of skills in each trade.
11. Updating the Laboratories and Library at the advice of Industrial Collaborators.
12. Accommodating the work skill classes to the time suited to Industrial Trainers and part time faculty members.
13. There must be a staff in the Community College to assist the Industrial Trainers to carry out Work Skill Programmes.
14. Neither student nor the college staff should count the time and duration of the classes or Work Skill Programmes, since this training is learner centred, flexible and totally dependent on the need of the community in which it is located.
15. Community College staff carry out the follow-up of the training in the college and in the industry very closely.
16. Community College should not count the cost, labour and pain but rather count the benefit of the excluded trainees in all aspects.
17. Parents' Meet is essential and is to be periodical to make the field placement a success and make the trainers really become employable.
18. Regular board of studies meeting is necessary and they are composed of Industrialists and Industrial Trainers.

What is to be Done? and What is not to be Done?

Community College efforts do not stop with one-time contacts or association. The Collaboration is continuous and college should never lose sight of the Role of Industrial and other related organisations. Genuineness, Truthfulness, Promptness, Regularity, Mutual Respect and Regular and Clear Communication are to be carefully attended with details, omitting anyone of these would result in strained relationship. Straining relationship in this collaboration will cost the employability of the excluded. Ultimately it will not serve the trainee and the Community.

Community College cannot function in strict frame of mind. Staff should update themselves to suit the need of the Community Management should be prepared to invest in the up-gradation of the faculty and in the welfare of the industrial trainers.

Conclusion

Community College is for People and people are to be motivated to understand the role of this College at regular intervals. Such association of the college with parents. Trainers and Partners from industries make the programmes relevant to the Industry, Community and to the Large Society, i.e. Nation. This Community College is built on Relationship, Collaboration and Co-ordination from Promotion of Employment, Entrepreneurs and Small-Scale Industrialists, finally the goal of Community College **"Empowerment of the Excluded"** is achieved through the above measures.

Dr. G.Pushparaj. S.J.
Director,
Madurai Community College
Tamilnadu

10.3 A Partnership with a Difference

One way to give a quality output is partnering with quality people. It is always a mutual beneficial ideology of betterment. The partnership of the Immaculate Community College of Cuddalore and Musee Educational group towards the unmatched contribution towards the unreached has a successful running of a year by now.

This model of an Educational Institution and an NGO working in the field of community enrichment using Training as the major tool has come together to make this conceptual dream a real one.

This model makes the following ideology come true:

- A Partnership with community consciousness
- A tie-up to break the religious fencing towards the community

- A model of institutional and NGO tie-up
- A perfect blend of Educational experience and Real Time experience

How the concept was well blended?

It had a simple truth in it, an Institution-Immaculate Sisters, with a legendry experience in conventional education, could understand the other side of the existing system of education.

The NGO reaching the grassroots people using its Training tool, which has an experience in moulding the people for living and not just existing, jointly tried various aspects of giving the "Best to the Least".

And exactly this blend started to work out. It exactly absorbed the concept of Community College System in India. This would certainly stand has a successful model in the system.

What are the other features of this model?

This would have also an Interesting answer in it, apart from the training partnership, the Musee Educational Group in its commercial expansion had a turn out of Industrial Partner also.

The Group has expanded in the areas of Computer Training Division – Targeting K-12 Business and Software Development. This expansion also very well helped in putting the real – time expectation of the market.

What is more innovative from us?

The other most ideal support is the Skill School Division of the Group. It works on Personality Development program for K-12 and for Colleges also. This wide experience had worked out in giving all the latest modules in the Soft Skill Development program to the Community College Students.

Since the group was working for quite a long time on Entrepreneurial Development program along with the Government agencies, it has made the group to introduce EDP programs to the students of Community College. It also working on a tie-up along with the District Industries Centre to consider the students with that appropriate training as beneficiaries also.

First time ever the group is working in the simulated program which is quite costly in the market and which is designed for MBA students.

The group also has designed management programs, which is likely to be introduced from the coming year of training.

The Purpose of this paper

Even though the paper has talked about the group at the outset, the inner urge towards this paper is the, recognition of the work of the force that has taken part in this movement all over the country.

Any thing in this world that matters would certainly need recognition in reaching the people. It might be an innovative concept on the shoulders of the western country, but this is more Indian-the traditional Gurukul System that has been poisoned by the western system needs an emerging out energy from the authorities for the simple reason of a result-oriented education.

This System with a technological backup could turn round the Indian Scenario, which is now making the world to look up on us. With one more blend of entrepreneurship we could also support the individual by which the Indian Economy could slowly balance itself.

- Paper presented to the Evaluation Team to the Community Colleges by Mr. S. Pugazhendhi, Concept Architect of Visions, Cuddalore, Tamilnadu

10.4 Industrial Partners Speak

Industrial Partners Speak:

Mr. B.T. Bangera, B.E., M.B.A., Managing Director, *Hi-Tech Arai Ltd., Madurai.*

Hi-Arai Ltd is a multinational Company a joint venture with M/S Arai Seisakusho Ltd., Japan, M/S Mitsubishi Corpn, Japan and M/S Japan International Development Organisation Ltd., Tokup. In 1990, this was tiny SSI family business with

annual turnover of Rs. 80 lacs per annum. In 2001 it has grown to Rs. 70 crore company employing over 580 employees. Achieving such phenomenal growth has been possible through people and with utmost focus of Human Resource Development.

In Madurai there is no dirth for manpower. If am not mistaken, we have more than a lakh of youth in Madurai as urban unemployed who have migrated from villages around Madurai. This is in addition to the local youth who pass out from ITI/ITC, SSC etc. every year.

In todays globalised environment with global competition, the only way to survive is by producing world class products for which we need to have world class employees. Unfortunately the regular stream of education, although imparts knowledge to the students, it does not impart appropriate work culture and mindset to produce quality product. By the time they are employed in the industry it is much too late for them to adapt to the work culture required.

It is in this context we turned our attention towards Madurai Community College when it was in the nascent stage and signed an MOU as an Industrial Partner. The idea was to associate with an educational Institute, which is not bogged down with age-old rules and regulations, inflexible teaching content and methods. Being a community college we wanted the institution to impart training which is relevant to the community in and around Madurai. It should be flexible enough to be in tune with changing times and needs with the least response time. As far as our Company is concerned we wanted MCC to help us in two ways.

(i) Convert the mindset of existing employees to fit into TQM philosophy to prepare them to face global competition.

(ii) To get readymade employees at the lowest level who should fit straightway into the existing work culture in the Organisation.

It is impossible to get these two aspects from the normal stream of education where focus on imparting appropriate work culture and quality is yet to be initiated.

There is a basic assumption running across the industry that the workmen are incapable of doing thinking part in their work and hence, they should mechanically do what is told to them. If we stick to this assumption, in this competitive era, the industry will have to lose its competitiveness irrespective of however good the technology is. It is here, we are using MCC to conduct tailor made programmes to the operators so that they think of TQM, zero defect, Total productive maintenance, Quality control circle movement, good house keeping Kaizen (continuous improvement) and develop leadership among workmen. As a result, today one of the four units with about 80 operators runs without any supervisor.

To spread this culture in the industry, we have even jointly with MCC developed a programme called Employee Competence development programme, which is otherwise not available in any kind of educational system.

As a good corporate citizen, we are also embarking on rural employment so that the migration from villages to Madurai can be confined. It is here we see a big role for MCC to train the young girls and boys in the villages according to employment that can be created by Industries.

I am *Senthilnathan*, Managing Director of *Premier System and Peripherals*. The staff of MCC are a link between their college and industry; and their service is appreciable. The students are trained to be well aware of the demand of the industry and

function accordingly. This service of MCC is laudable and we, the industrialists, are privileged to be associated with the social service of MCC.

I am *M. Joseph*, Proprietor of *Zion Refrigeration*. I am proud of my association with this college from it inception in 1997. I am, besides being its industrial partner and a member of the Advisory Body from 1998 and also serving as a visiting faculty of

Madurai Community College from 2000 onwards. I see MCC as an extraordinary college for the academically, economically and socially disadvantaged groups. I see a vast difference in the Director, Administrator and the faculty in their ways of teaching and counseling and their approaches towards students every day to see their friendly approaches.

I am *D. Ramasamy*, Chief Executive Officer of *'E Plus Plus'* in Madurai, providing sales and services of Computers for the past 10 years. Madurai Community College, an ISO 9001-2000

Certified institute, provides high standard of technical knowledge with ways and means living the art of life. It organizes field Training and job-placement for the target group and it is praise worthy.

I, *Er.S.Rajasekaran*, Managing Director, *Susee Car and Trucks Pvt. Ltd.*, know the concept of Community College famous

in U.S. and England. It is planted in Madurai with the guidance of Rev. Fr. Dr. Xavier Alphonse, S.J., and Rev. Fr. Dr. Pushparaj, S.J., for the first time in Madurai.

I, *L. Murali Krishnan*, Managing Director, *Kalayani Associates Pvt, Ltd.*, (Group). I am associated with MCC for the past three years. We, the authorized dealer of Honda, find our

association with MCC to attain perfection by giving an opportunity to their trainees and it is a contribution to the society. We have also passed a resolution in the Board Meeting that any further recruitments and requirements shall be fulfilled through MCC. We wish this celestial service to the community should continue.

I am *G. Elango*, Proprietor of *Sai Engineering Company*. Our company finds it a great pleasure to be associated with MCC. This college is much better than any other college in the city because it educates the school drop outs, X std and college students. Even the best colleges do not do this.

I am *Jaffer M. Patel*, General Manger of *Madura Park Inn.* The field training held in Hotels for the student trainees of MCC turns the less confident to be well-motivated and confident. They evince a lot of team spirit and are capable of confronting hard realities of life. Our Hotel has come forward to place Mr. Julius Conrad and Mr. Arul John Kennedy.

Madurai Community College, April 1997

SCAD Community College, April 1998

Chennai Corporation Community College, December 1998

St. Aloysius Community College, (MoU), Jabalpur, Madhya Pradesh, July 2004

11

Self Employment

11.1 Self-Employment Opportunities available.

1. Mini Bakery
2. Spices and Curry Powder
3. Sugarcane Juice Stall
4. Packed Lunch
5. Fried Products
6. Cold Food Stall
7. Potato / Banana Wafers
8. Pickles and Condiments
9. Tamarind Pulp
10. Sago Rings
11. Fruit Juice Stall
12. Soft Ice Cream
13. Vermicelli
14. Coffee Roasting and Grinding
15. Popcorn
16. Papad Making
17. Groundnut Decorticator
18. Confectionery
19. Peanut Candy
20. Salt Grinding
21. Grinding of Cereals / Spices

22. Prawn Pickle
23. Cleaning Powder
24. Wax Candle
25. Agarbatti
26. Liquid Detergent
27. Boot Polish
28. Camphor Tablets
29. White Phenoyle
30. Fountain pen Ink
31. Laundry Soap
32. Hair Oil
33. Plastic Articles
34. PVC Diary Cover
35. Nail Polish
36. Rubber Stamp Ink
37. Market Information Services
38. Advertising Agency
39. Communication Services
40. Clinical Laboratory
41. Tent House
42. Child Care Centre
43. Typewriting Institute
44. Book Lending Library
45. Sub Contract Business to Export Houses
46. Software Consultancy
47. Fast Food Stall
48. Marriage Bureau
49. Printing Press
50. General Engineering Services
51. Laundry Cum Sari Starching Centre
52. Function Arrangement agency
53. Residential Service Centre
54. Investment / Financial Service Centre

55. Industrial Clearing Service Centre
56. Architecture Consultancy
57. Wood Planning
58. Automobile Servicing
59. Lamination of Identity Cards and Documents
60. Beauty Parlor / Health Club
61. Knitted Leather Belt
62. Gents Hand Bags
63. Pouch From Foam
64. Ladies Hand Bags
65. Cemented Type Chappal
66. Ladies Sandal
67. Shoes
68. Leather Laces
69. Aluminum Slug Stock
70. Cycle Stand and Carriers
71. Aluminum Utensils
72. Builders Hardware (Hinges)
73. Simple Pressed Components
74. Auto Silencers
75. Agricultural Implements
76. Gage Servicing
77. Luggage Carriers and Scooter Baskets
78. Steel Furniture and Fabrication
79. Wooden Doors and Windows
80. Carpentry
81. Brick for Building
82. Building Lime
83. Concrete Jalli / Pundi
84. Decoration of Pottery / Crockery
85. Decorative Clay Models
86. Mosaic Tiles
87. Polished Stone Blocks

88. Screen Printing
89. Slate Pencils
90. Spectacle Lenses
91. Synthetic Gem Cutting
92. Socks
93. Petticoats
94. Brassieres and Pillow Covers
95. Sanitary Napkins
96. Small transformers
97. Automobile Cartridge Fuses
98. Fluorescent Tube Light Chokes
99. Electronic Fan Regulators and Light Dimmer
100. Battery Charging and Reconditioning
101. Electronic Intercom System
102. Electronic Gas Lighter
103. Domestic Electronic Timer
104. Emergency Lamps
105. Battery Chargers
106. Electronic Door Bells
107. T. V. Servicing
108. Assembling of Audio Cassettes
109. T. V. Antennas
110. Wire Wound Resistors
111. Assembling of Starters of Fluorescent Lamps
112. Soft Solder
113. House and Commercial Wiring
114. Link Clip for Electric Wiring
115. Brushes for Paint, Industrial and Sanitary uses
116. Industrial Gloves
117. Wallet and Key Chains
118. Suitcase and Attach Cases

11.2 Loans Available from Various Banks

1. **IFCI** – Industrial Finance Corporation of India
2. **TIIC** – Tamilnadu Industrial Investment Corporation
3. **IDBI** – Industrial Development Bank of India
4. **NSIC** – National Small Industries Corporation Ltd.,
5. **ICICI** – Industrial Credit and Investment Corporation of India
6. **IRCI** – Industrial Reconstruction Corporation of India Ltd.,
7. **SDFC** – Shipping Development Fund Committee
8. **NB** – National Bank
9. **ECGC** – Export Credit and Guarantee Corporation Ltd.,
10. **UTI** – Unit Trust of India
11. **LIC** – Life Insurance Corporation Ltd.,
12. **GICI** – General Insurance Corporation of India
13. **SIDCO** – Tamilnadu Small Industrial Development Corporation
14. **SISI** – Small Industries Service Institute
15. District Industries Centre
16. Regional District Directorate of Industries and Commerce
17. State Industries Promotion Corporation of Tamilnadu
18. Minerals and Metals Trading Corporation of India Ltd.,
19. State Trading Corporation
20. Steel Authority of India

11.3 Case Studies

Case I

Name	:	Mr. G. Sathya,
Age	:	45 Years
Educational Qualification	:	B. Sc (Maths)
Occupation	:	Xerox, STD, Couriers, Spiral Binding, Typewriting, Video and Still, Photography, Sellers of Law Books, Screen-Printing, etc.
Investment	:	Rs. One Lakh
Monthly Income	:	Rs. 20, 000 /-
Annual Income	:	Rs. 2,40,000 /-
No. of Employees	:	5 Persons
Address	:	Shop No. 8, TNSCB Complex, 212, R. K. Mutt Road, Chennai – 600 028. Ph: 461 8722

Mr. G. Sathya is an Enthusiastic Entrepreneur. He is a Science Graduate at present. He is the owner of Xerox Shop, DTP works, Photo and Video Coverage, Printing Work, etc. He had invested Rupees One Lakh in his Business. At present he has five employees working under him. His monthly income is minimum of Rs. 20,000.

Feedback

He strongly believes in Vivekananda's Proverb *"No Pain No Gain"*. He feels that hard work is very important in life, which leads to the path of Success. Chastity and Charity lead to permanent Prosperity. Punctuality and Honesty is the secret behind every successful man.

Case II

Name	:	Mr. Govinda Kumar,
Age	:	21 Years
Educational Qualification	:	10th Std.,
Occupation	:	Sugarcane Juice
Investment	:	Rs. 30,000 /-
Monthly Income	:	Rs. 3,000 /-
Annual Income	:	Rs. 36,000 /-
No. of Employees	:	2 Persons
Address	:	R. K. Mutt Road, Chennai – 600 028.

Mr. Govinda Kumar is an Entrepreneur. He hails from a very poor family. He has passed only 10th standard from Government Higher Secondary School at Thiruvanamalai District. He owns a Sugarcane Juice Stall at R. K. Mutt Road, Chennai. He has invested around Rs. 30,000 /- three years ago with the help of his parents. His daily income is Rs. 100. Now he has two branches one at 70 feet road Perambur and at Ayanavaram. He has two employees working under him.

Feedback

Per day he sells Juice for three bundles of Sugarcane. He spends Rs. 35 for each bundle. His customers are of different class groups. He charges Rs. 4 for each glass of Juice. From survival point of view this business is good. But only large-scale business will fetch more profit. Everybody can start this business and hard work will bring great success.

Case III

Name	:	Mr. R. Muthu
Age	:	29 Years
Educational Qualification	:	9th Standard
Occupation	:	Fast Food
Investment	:	Rs. 15,000 /-
Monthly Income	:	Rs. 9,000 /- to 10,000/-
Annual Income	:	Rs. 1,20,000 /-
No. of Employees	:	2 Persons
Address	:	Thangaval Fast Food, 158, Nungambakkam High Road, Chennai – 600 034.

Mr. R. Muthu is an active and self motivated Entrepreneur who has passed his 9th Standard. He is in this business for the past three years and earns Rs. 300/- Rs. 400/- per day. His investment was around Rupees Fifteen Thousand. Under him two male workers with good experience in the same field are working. He also takes Catering Order for private parties, marriage etc.

Case IV

Name	:	Mr. A. Joshi
Age	:	55 Years
Educational Qualification	:	M. Sc
Occupation	:	Manufacturing Noodles
Investment	:	Rs. 5,000 /-
Monthly Income	:	Rs. 3,000 /- Rs. 4,000 /-
Annual Income	:	Rs. 40,000 /-
No. of Employees	:	Son, Wife involved in this business as a full time Employee.
Address	:	80, Behind Zambazar Market, Triplicane, Chennai – 600 005.

Mr. A. Joshi is a Post Graduate from Presidency College, Chennai. He manufactures noodles and supplies to the retail provision shops in and around Chennai. His keen interest in business has brought him to this field. He earns around Rs. 100- to Rs. 200 /- per day. His son takes care of the marketing of the product.

11.4 Proposal for Self Employment - Garage Service

Introduction

Automobile service centre is very important these days. Because of the rapid growth of automobile both two and four wheelers in the modern world, automobile maintenance is possible. Automobile service centre is a profitable business.

Raw Material

Raw material in the sense Screw Driver, Nail, Grease, Lubricant Oil, Paints etc.

Demand and Supply

Past two years motor cycles production is high so a lot of demand for garage servicing centres.

Practical

Annual Target - Rs. 1,80,000 /-
Land - Used Space – 20 sq.ft.,
Building - Rental Space / monthly Rs. 1,000 /-

Equipment	Value in Rs.
1. Air Compressor 1 HP Motor	9,000.00
2. Drilling Machine 12 mm	2,500.00
3. DW Table Sharpener Wheel 150 mm HP Motor	3,000.00
4. Gas Welding Set	6,500.00
5. Screw Jack	800
6. Handling Equipment	2,000.00
7. Rubber Tube, Welgunising Equipment	2,000.00
8. Office Equipment	1,500.00
TOTAL	30,800.00

Salary and Wage

Worker	Number	Salary in Rs.	TOTAL
Skilled Worker	3	750.00	2,250.00
Helper	5	400.00	2,000.00
TOTAL			4,250.00

Other Expenditure

Rent	- Rs. 1,000.00
Other Expenditure	- Rs. 1,000.00
Total	*- Rs. 2,000.00*

Total Current Investment

Monthly Expenditure	- Rs. 12,500.00

Total Capital

Machine and Allied Equipment	- Rs. 30,800.00
Current Capital	- Rs. 12,250.00

Annual Production Expenditure

Total Capital	- Rs. 1,47,000.00
Wear and Tear	- Rs. 3,000.00
Interest	- Rs. 4,300.00
Total	*- Rs.1,54,380.00*
Annual Sales	*- Rs. 1,80,000.00*
Annual Profit	*- Rs. 25,620.00*
Annual Sales	*- Rs. 17 %*
Employment	
Opportunity	- 8

Machine and Associate Seller

1. Armstrong Smith & Co, 45, Armenian Street, Chennai – 600 001
2. Raja Machine Tools, 91, Thambu Chetty Street, Chennai – 600 001
3. N G Equipment, 40 Pantheon road, Egmore, Chennai – 600 008.
4. India Machine Tools & Co., Chennai – 600 001.
5. Gujarat Machine Tools, 135 Lingi Chetty Street, Chennai – 600 001.

• *Thanks to Chennai Need Analysis Team of MCRDCE.*

12

Administration and Governance of Community Colleges

12.1 Administration and Governance of Community Colleges

The Community College will ensure the participation of the members of the agency that establishes the Community College (Board of Management), Administrators, Representatives of the faculty of the Community College, Industrial Partners, Community Leaders, Consultants to the Community College and Representatives nominated by the Government.

The authorities of the College will make sure of the proper management of Life Skills, Work Skills Development, Placement for Training, Financial and General administrative matters and also the needed infrastructural facilities necessary for training. The structure of the Governance of the Community Colleges will be the following:

Statutory Bodies

I. Board of Management
II. Governing Body of the College
III. Advisory Council

12.2 Statutory Bodies

Community College will have the following three statutory Bodies.

I. Board of Management
II. Governing Body of the College
III. Advisory Council

I. Board of Management

The agency that owns and establishes the Community College.

Functions

(1) It ensures the specific identity and orientation of Community College

(2) It lays down policies and guidelines.

(3) It undertakes planning and funding and allocation of resources.

(4) Monitors the functioning of the Community College according to the philosophy of the Community College System.

II. Governing Body

Representatives of Board of Management, Industrial Partners, Faculty Members, Administrators, Community Leaders and Consultants to the Community College and one representative appointed by the State Government.

Functions

(1) Approves the budget

(2) Obtains an appraisal of the functioning of the college.

(3) Awards Diplomas and Certificates to the candidates declared eligible by the College.

III. Advisory Council

It Consists of Community Leaders, Industrial Partners and Faculty Members of the College.

Functions

(1) It helps in the Need Analysis.

(2) It designs the Curriculum.

(3) It validates the Evaluation and Assessment of Skills.

(4) It helps in the planning of the relevant courses.

(5) It advises on the Job Placement.

(6) It suggests means of fund-raising.

12.3 Administrative Structure - Day To Day Administration

(A Suggested Model)

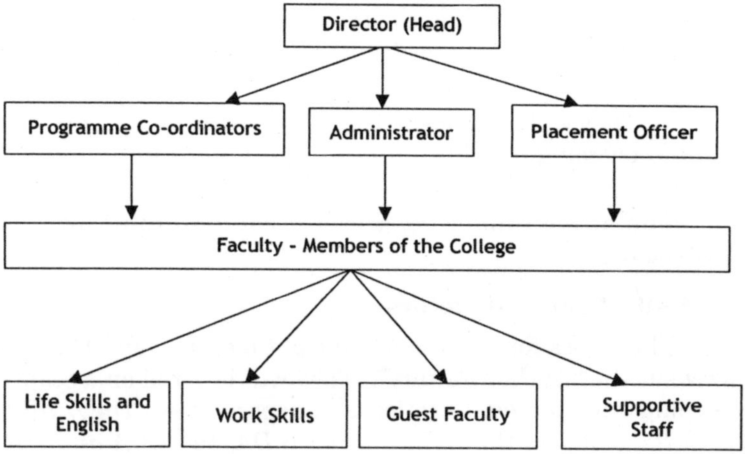

- Each Community College will function as an antonomus unit, supervised by the *Community College Development Agency.*
- What is envisaged in the Governance of the Community College is Minimum Control, Maximum Room and Freedom for Growth and Innovation in response to the local needs of the community towards the promotion of skills for the underprivileged and in catering to the excluded target groups eliminated from the formal system.

12.4 The Qualification of the Instructors, Salary of the Instructors and Service Conditions

Faculty members of the Community College can be divided into three categories, *Full Time Instructors, Part Time Instructors and Guest Faculty.*

(a) Selection and Training

- Qualified Post-graduates and Under Graduates are selected on the basis of aptitude test.
- They will be chosen on the basis of their competence

and commitment to the mission of the Community College.

- They are given special training with a Diploma in Community College Teaching with a minimum of 12 weeks of training conducted by the *Madras Centre for Research and Development of Community Education (MCRDCE), Chennai.*
- They will undergo periodical performance appraisal and on going training.

The above conditions are applicable to the Full Time Instructors.

(b) Full - Time Instructors

They work for a minimum of eight hours a day. They will serve as the "Anchor Faculty". They will be fixed on a scale in keeping with the qualification and experiences. They will be paid *Rs. 3,500* as the *Basic Pay* with *DA, PF, CCA and HRA* according to the rules of the State Government. Their continuation in service as well as increment in pay will depend on the performance appraisal earlier mentioned.

(c) Part - Time Instructors

Part - Time Instructors will be from the respective fields of specialisation with the years of experience in the field and with the knowledge of the skills required for the jobs for which the Community College trains its students even though they may not have formal academic degrees.

They will be paid on an hourly basis. They will also go through periodic training in the imparting of skills.

(d) Guest Faculty

They will be invited to take special sessions in their areas of expertise and they will be paid according to the local conditions.

(e) Supporting Staff

Supporting Staff will provide the management the necessary service for efficient administration and delivery of the Community College System.

They will start with Rs. 2,000 as their Basic Pay with the DA, PF, CCA and HRA according to the State Government Rules.

12.5 Registers and Information to be kept by the Community College

The following registers and information is to be maintained by the Community College:

1. Document of the Need Analysis of the Local Area
2. Admission Register of the College.
3. Attendance Register of the Students and the Staff.
4. Acquittance register of the teaching staff and the non-teaching staff.
5. Master mark register of all the skills and work skills courses and the certification from the Industrial supervisors.
6. Portfolio of every individual student with all the details about the student and his or her career.
7. Inventory register of all the equipment and library books.
8. The list of successful candidates and the job placement directory of every batch.
9. The detailed curriculum of Life Skills and Job oriented Programmes.
10. The accounts register of the College.
11. The list of Industrial Partners and the Bio-data of the Industrial Partners.
12. The Memorandum of Understanding or letters of consent for collaboration with the Industrial Partners.
13. The minutes of the Governing Board and The Advisory Board meetings.
14. The Diary of events of the College.

12.6 Expectations from the Government

1. **Recognition and Approval** of the Community College System and the courses offered by the Community Colleges.

2. **Indirect Financial Assistance** could be had from

   (i) Rural Development Department

(ii) Social Welfare Department

(iii) Health Department

(iv) Women Welfare / Empowerment Department

(v) Youth Welfare and Sports Department

(vi) The Quasi Government Organisations / Public Sector Agencies to ensure placements.

(vii) Funds of the *Special Component Plan* Programmes for the welfare of the SC / ST Population.

3. Direct Financial Assistance

(i) Institution of Scholarships and subsidised tuition fees

(ii) Issue of free Bus / Railway Passes

(iii) Subsidised Canteen Facility

(iv) Provision of learning Aids / Equipment to students

4. Maintenance of Separate Employment Register / Placement Register.

5. Creation of an Autonomous Community Development Board to ensure quality and monitoring.

6. Abstaining from imposing Direct Governmental Restrictions.

13

Recognition and Accreditation of Community Colleges

Various Efforts at Recognition

April 1997	The *Madras Community College* started its efforts for Recognition with the Government of Tamil Nadu.
July 1998	*First Consultation* of Community Colleges, Madurai to help the MS University, Tirunelveli to understand the nature, philosophy and functioning of the Community College System. First Effort at the Articulation of the System *(7 Community Colleges).*
January 1999	First South Indian Conference of Community Colleges, Chennai, Establishment of MCRDCE – Awareness among Educationists, Teachers and Administrators of Community Colleges, Community Leaders, Potential Employers about the Community College System – An understanding of the Indian Community College System in contrast with the Systems in USA, UK, Australia and Germany. (14 Existing and 10 Upcoming Community Colleges)
March 1999	Second Consultation of Community Colleges, Madurai, Evolving Self

	Regulatory Guidelines to be submitted to the Government of Tamil Nadu for Recognition and Approval of the System. (12 Existing and 9 Upcoming Community Colleges).
October 1999	Third Consultation of Community Colleges at the direction of the Secretary of Higher Education, Government of Tamil Nadu and Submission of the Document for Recognition to the Government of Tamil Nadu – Document referred to the Director of Collegiate Education and he submits the document with his comments. (18 Existing and 6 Upcoming Community Colleges).
October 1999	Submission of the Document for Recognition and Approval of Community Colleges by the Government of Tamil Nadu to Mr. Selvam, IAS, Education Secretary, Government of Tamil Nadu.
February 2000	National Workshop on Community College System in collaboration with the HRD Ministry, New Delhi at Chennai in which the Community Colleges, a number of NGOs and a dozen HRD Officials participated. The System gets national approval. (13 Existing Community Colleges and 46 NGOs)
November 2000	In the 31st meeting of the Tamil Nadu State Council for Higher Education a recommendation was made as follows: *"Since there is scope and demand for a variety of skill associated Programmes with opportunities for ready employment not only for those who have completed +2 but also those with 8th Std and 10th Std qualifications, it was resolved further to recommend to the Government the need*

to encourage such Programmes and to establish an autonomous body for streamlining the establishment of institutions offering skill development courses"

- Mr.Kaw, IAS, Education Secretary, MHRD, Government of India requests Mr.Manivanan, IAS, Education Secretary, Government of Tamilnadu and Prof. D.Victor, Former Director of Collegiate Education, Government of Tamilnadu to issue the GO as quickly as possible in October 2000. The Director of MCRDCE meets Mr. Manivanan, IAS on 15th of Sept 2000, 2nd of January 2001, 27th of February 2001 regarding recognition.
- A high level meeting was called by the Chief Secretary of Tamil Nadu on the 20th of February 2001 with the heads of the Departments of Education and no decision was taken with the regard to the GO.

March 2001 — National Consultation on Community College System with Lokabodhan Kendra in Collaboration with HRD Ministry, New Delhi at Indian Social Institute, New Delhi from 17 States of India. The request was made to the Education Secretary, Government of India to recognize the system at the national level. (23 Existing Community Colleges).

2001 April — Fourth Consultation of Community Colleges - A Follow-up of the National Consultation on the Community College System in India in which Dr. K. Venkatasubramanian, Member, Union Planning Commission, New Delhi participated. (23 Existing Community Colleges).

- A request letter for Appointment to discuss the Recognition and Approval was submitted on 7th of July 2001 to Mr.Mohan Verghese Chunkath, IAS, the New Secretary of Education, Government of Tamil Nadu.

13th July 2001 — Meeting Mr. Mohan Verghese Chunkath, IAS, New Secretary of Education, Government of Tamil Nadu and no conclusion was reached. The New Secretary needed more time to examine the documents.

Visit of the Review Team appointed by NCERT - 16th to 23rd of July 2001

Visit of Dr. M. Sen Gupta, Head, Humanities, Science and Education Division, Pandit Sunderlal Sharma Central Institute of Vocational Education, Bhopal and Dr. Duraisamy, Professor and Head, Regional Institute of Education, Mysore nominated members of National Council for Education Research and Training (NCERT), New Delhi to do the evaluation of Eight Community Colleges and submitted an official report to the Government of India.

National Institute of Open Schooling

11th October 2001 — Meeting Dr. Sangal, Director (Academic), NOS and Dr. Abhay Kumar, Vocational Education Unit, NOS

- Meeting Prof. N.K. Ambasht, Chairman, NOS and submitting the letter of request on behalf of all Community Colleges for Recognition and Accreditation- Dr.Abhay Kumar, Coordinator, NOS appointed for the project.

2001 December — Fifth Consultation on Recognition and Accreditation of Community Colleges in India, in particular to National Institute of Open Schooling (NIOS) and Indira Gandhi National Open University

(IGNOU), New Delhi and the modality and procedure of accreditation discussed. (27 Existing Community Colleges).

Statement of the Consultation

Taking into account the advantages of asking for Recognition and Accreditation from the NOS, the assembly endorses the attempts made by MCRDCE to get Recognition from the NOS. It authorizes the MCRDCE to negotiate with the appropriate bodies to get Recognition and work out the practical modalities that are involved in this process.

The assembly reiterates that at no point of time, the Mission and Vision of Community College should be sacrificed in this process. The target group should be always kept in mind. They are the marginalised of the society who do not enjoy the benefits of Higher Education.

Accreditation to NIOS

- As a result of the Fifth Consultation 18 Community Colleges were Accredited to National Institute of Open Schooling in the last two years.

Union Planning Commission

Mention in the document of the Tenth five-year Plan:

> *"There should be focus on convergence of schemes like the Sarva Shiksha Abhiyan, Adult Education and Vocational Education Programme at Schools, ITIs, Polytechnics, Community Colleges etc."*

(Tenth Five Year Plan (2002 -2007), Chapter 2.4 Vocational Education p. 51).

2003 July	Sixth Consultation of Community Colleges in India at Chennai, Madurai, Trichy and Tirunelveli. (162 Participants from 55 Community Colleges)

Issues emerged during the Consultation

1. Recognition from State and Central Governments.
2. Central Placement Cell in Collaboration with Confederation of Indian Industries and Chambers of Commerce.

3. Soliciting Government Funds Stipends and Scholarships.
4. Approaching IGNOU, NIOS for Accreditation.
5. Approaching IGNOU, NIOS for Accreditation.
6. International Collaboration – Networking with Association of American Community Colleges through MCRDCE.
7. Target Group to be sharpened.

National Minorities Education Commission

August 2004	A Project Proposal towards Recognition of the Community College System all over India, Stipends and Scholarships to students, MCRDCE to be approved by MHRD as an Institute for Community Colleges as it was recommended by the National Consultation in March 2001.
September 2004	Seventh Consultation of Community Colleges (70 Participants from 45 Community Colleges). Dialogue is started with TNOU for Recognition and Accreditation. Prof. M.S. Palanichamy, Vice Chancellor initiates the Dialogue. A draft memorandum is submitted to the Vice Chancellor.

- Members of the National Minorities Education Commission hand over the Proposal to Shri. Arjun Singh, Minister for Human Resource Development on the 27th of August 2004. Response is awaited from the Ministry.
- First Meeting of the National Committee on Community Colleges held at MHRD, Shastri Bhavan, New Delhi on 28th of February 2005.
  - **The following members were present**
    - Shri Sudeep Banerjee, Additional Secretary - Chairperson, Ministry of HRD, Department of (S&HE)
    - Prof. H.P. Dixit, Vice-Chancellor
      Indira Gandhi National Open University and Chairperson
      All India Council of Technical Education

- Shri Sunil Kumar, Joint Secretary (Higher Education)

  Ministry of HRD, Department of (S&HE)
- Prof.Ved Prakash, Secrtary

  University Grants Commission
- Dr. Xavier Alphonse, Director

  Madras Center for Research and Development

  in Community Education
- Dr. D.K. Paliwal, Deputy Education Adviser
  Ministry of HRD, Department of (S&HE)

- The Second meeting of the National Committee was held on the 10th of May 2005 in which all the Government agencies that are offering Vocational Programme were invited to work out the equivalence of credits that could be integrated into the main stream of Higher Education.

February 2005	Seminar and Workshop on Indian Community College System, held at University of Madras, organised by University of Madras and US Consulate General, Chennai on the 8th and 9th of February 2005. (63 Participants from 43 Community Colleges)
March 2005	Fourth National Consultation of Community Colleges in India, held at Asha Nivas, Chennai on the 11th and 12th of March 2005. (86 Existing Community Colleges and 24 Upcoming Community Colleges from 14 States of India).
20th August 2005	Eighth Consultation of Community Colleges in Tamil Nadu with the Tamil Nadu Open University – Integration of Tamil Nadu Open University Diploma Courses with the Community College System (93 Participants from 54 Community Colleges). 78 Community Colleges are recognised as Vocational Programme Centres of TNOU.

October 2005	Ninth Consultation of Community Colleges in India, 14th and 15th of October 2005 at Chennai (47 Participants from 30 Community Colleges). The recognition is extended to Community Colleges in other parts of India by TNOU.

14

The Contribution of MCRDCE to the Community College Movement in India

14. The Contribution of MCRDCE to the Community College Movement in India

14.1 The Origin

The Community College movement started in India in 1995. As the Community Colleges were emerging there was the need felt by the Colleges to have a coordinating agency. To respond to this need The Madras Centre for Research and Development of Community Education (MCRDCE) was started in January 1999. It is an undertaking of the Jesuits of Tamil Nadu Province to help and serve the Community College Movement.

14.2 The Objectives of MCRDCE

- To Include the Excluded
- Giving the Best to the
- Matching Education with Employment.
- Close Linkage with Industries
- Thc Participation of the Community
- The Development of Skills and Competencies
- Enhancing the Employability

14.3 The Activities of MCRDCE

- To respond to the dynamism of the Community College Movement in India.
- To provide a resource centre with books and study materials.

- To help in the process of curriculum development
- To have training Programmes for the Community College teachers and administrators
- To evolve methods of evaluation and assessment of skills
- To publish books and articles
- To popularise the concept all over the country
- To help in the preparation of Community Colleges
- To document the process and evolution of the Community College Movement
- To influence the State and Central Governments, Universities and the UGC, to recognise and accept the Community College System as an educational alternative
- To replicate the model all over the country with the help of the Human Resource Development Ministry, New Delhi.
- To enter into International networking of Community Colleges in USA, UK, Germany, Australia, South Africa and Canada.

14.4 The Contribution of MCRDCE

1. ***Community College Teachers Training Programmes from all over India***
   - Total Number of Training Programmes conducted : 16
   - Total Number of Participants : 951
   - Total Number of Organisation : 394

2. ***Community College Teachers Training Programme on Life Coping Skills***
   - Total Number of Training Programmes conducted : 2
   - Total Number of Participants : 99
   - Total Number of Organisations : 68

3. ***Regional Workshops***
   - Total Number of Workshops : 39
   - Total Number of Participants : 1,728
   - Total Number of Organisations : 759

4. *National Workshops on Community College System in India*

In collaboration with HRD Ministry, New Delhi

- No. of National Workshop : 04
- Total Number of Organisations : 270
- Total Number of Participants : 582

5. *Consultations among Community Colleges*

- Total Number of Consultations : 24
- Total Number of Participants : 1218
- Total Number of Organisation : 389

6. *Consultation on the Profile of the Rural Community College*

- Total Number of Consultations : 6
- Total Number of Participants : 318
- Total Number of Organisations : 132

7. *Consultation for the Tsunami Affected People*

- Total Number of Consultations : 5
- Total Number of Students : 1,616

8. *MCRDCE and NGOs in India*

- MCRDCE has worked with 800 NGOs in 23 States.

9. *Resource Material and Documentation available at MCRDCE*

1. *Life Skills* - Detailed syllabus for Life Coping Skills, Interpersonal Relationship and Communication Skills, Basic Computer Applications and Developmental English.
2. *Work Skills* - Detailed syllabus for Hotel Management and Office Technology.
3. Curriculum outline available for 28 Work skills Programme
4. *978 books* available on Life Skills, Communication Skills, Developmental English and various Work skills.

5. Documentation on the History of the Community College.

(Newspaper Clippings - 500, Videotapes - 100, Audiotapes - 64 and Photographs – 7,217)

10. Publications: Books and Articles.
Books

1. *Changing Track* - Community Colleges in India, December 1996, Second Edition, June 2001.
2. An Introduction to the Community College System (Tamil), September 1998.
3. *Including the Excluded* - History of the Community Colleges in India, January 1999.
4. *Autonomous Colleges in India* - History, Performance and Future, February 2000.
5. *People Building Business* - Proceedings of the National Workshop on Community College System, October 2000.
6. *A Community College Movement*: A National Phenomenon of the National Consultation on Community College System in India, March 2001.
7. *Reaching Out*: Community College Movement in India - An Update, July 2001.
8. The Contribution of MCRDCE in the Community College in India, December 2001.
9. *Mismatch*: Establishing and Developing Community Colleges in India, MCRDCE Publication, Chennai, June 2002.
10. *We Shall Overcome* : A Textbook on Life Coping Skills, MCRDCE Publication, Chennai March 2004.
11. *Best to the Least* : Profile of Community Colleges in India, MCRDCE Publication, Chennai November 2004.
12. *Walking the Extra Mile* : A textbook on Interpersonal Relationship and Communication Skills, MCRDCE Publication, Chennai, March 2005.
13. *Computer Made Easy* : A textbook on Basic Computing Skills, MCRDCE Publication, Chennai, March 2005.

14. *Miracles of Hope* : Success Stories of Community College Students, MCRDCE Publication, Chennai, March 2005.
15. *Marching with the Marginalised* : The Contribution of MCRDCE to the Community College Movement in India (1995-2005), MCRDCE Publication, Chennai, December 2005.
16. *Community College Empowerment Endorsed* : The History of Recognition and Accreditation of Community Colleges in India (1995-2005), MCRDCE Publication, Chennai, December 2005.
17. *Bloom and Blossom* : A Source Book on Eco Friendly sustainable Agriculture for Integrated Rural Development, MCRDCE Publication, Chennai, December 2005.

Articles

- New Frontiers in Education, USA - 10
- University News - 13
- Varia - 9
    - The Community College Times
    - The Hindu
    - AIACHE Newsletter
    - Education world
    - The Economic Times
    - News Today
    - Total number of articles published - 31

15

Profile of the Rural Community College

15.1 Introduction

There is the urgent need to link Agriculture and Rural Development with Education for Livelihood and Skills Development. Due to the new emerging trends in Agricultural Farming and Rural Developmental Approaches to reach up to International standards, there is the need for the enhancement of Human Recourses and the developmental of newer and updating of skills. There is also the urgent necessity of harnessing the human resources and manpower of the Rural Community. This fits in well with the search of the Community College Movement.

15.2 What is a Rural Community College?

- Rural Community College has arisen as an urgent requirement for empowering the rural people through skills education for self-employment as well as group employment in rural areas.

15.3 The Features of Rural Community College

- Meets the needs of the local community
- People participating and people benefiting
- Aims at capacity building of rural people
- Improves talents of youth
- Taps resources and potentialities in rural areas.
- Provides skills for self-employment
- Creates job opportunities for eradicating poverty
- More field oriented with practical inputs

- Trains rural youth in traditional sectors.
- Enhances collaboration between government and service sector.
- Facilitates self-reliant initiatives in rural areas.
- Makes interested youth to upscale their education and skills
- Transforms the qualitative aspects of life of the rural poor
- Initiates sustainable livelihood options for poverty alleviation
- Empowers rural people through integrated development

15.4 Rationale for the Promotion of a Rural Community College

There is a great need for people, especially the young to discover great meaning and dignity in their lives and find positive, healthy, productive alternatives to unemployment, isolation, boredom, alienation, addiction and violence. Over 72% of the population in rural areas are not able to make a decent living mainly because of regular employment and income generation. Hence, creating gainful employment opportunities is the biggest challenge today.

The opportunities for regular employment and income generation in rural areas can be grouped into on-farm and off-farm activities. Initially, the agro-based activities cannot provide adequate opportunities for the landless laborers. But, subsequently, with the optimum use of resources and enhanced productivity, demand for labour will rise and even the landless will have increased employment opportunities with improvement in agriculture productivity, job opportunities for ancillary services will also increase and hereto, the landless laborers can take advantage of the situation. Based on the above rural development focus two community colleges have been started in Siruganur, Tamilnadu and Lachragarh, Jharkhand

TWO MODELS

15.5 Lachragarh, Jharkhand

Montfort Community College is run by the Montfort Brothers of St. Gabriel, Ranchi Province. It is hoped that Montfort

Community College would come up with a new educational system against the present system learning and give options to those who cannot progress in life due to poverty, weakness and injustice in the society. Therefore Community College aims at full development of those unemployed youth who cannot complete or cannot go to school. Community College will provide work efficiency to more youth every year which will give them much confidence to live prestigious life in the society and provide them the atmosphere for job opportunities. The institute will also provide them with a moral education and leadership programmes so as to form a good society.

15.6 Courses Conducted by the Rural Community College

1. Tailoring
2. Motor Mechanic
3. Carpentry
4. Welding
5. Masonry
6. Agriculture

15.7 Ertram Rural Community College

Ertram Rural Community College is situated at the Human Resource Development Training Centre of VOICE Trust at Siruganur village in Mannachanallur Block, Trichy District, State of Tamil Nadu, South India.

Siruganur is 25 kilometers north of Trichy in the Trichy-Chennai National Highways (NH 45). It is linked by bus transportation between Trichy and Perambalur, the District Head Quarters of the neighbouring district of Perambalur at a distance of 30 kilometers north of Siruganur.

Siruganur is a village Panchayat of Mannachanallur block which has 156 villages big and small. It is one of the 38 village Panchayats of Mannachanallur Block.

Voice Trust (Voice for the Oppressed through Integrated Community Emancipation) was registered in 1985 under Trust act as a Non Profit and Voluntary Organisation. Being a NGO, VOICE Trust is involving in various social action initiatives for the disadvantaged groups of people especially, women, children, landless, small farmers, unemployed youth, the disabled, the destitute and the ageing.

15.8 Courses Conducted by this Community College

1. Diploma in Sustainable Farming Systems for Integrated Rural Development
2. Diploma in Pre- Primary Teacher Training
3. Diploma in House Electrician
4. Diploma in DTP Operator

5. Diploma in Plumbing Technology
6. Diploma in Fashion Designing & Garment Making

16

The Role of Universities

16.1 Introduction

The Community College Movement has been growing in India during the last ten years. It was aimed primarily at the socio economic weaker and disadvantaged sections of the society leading to empowerment through skills development thus providing education for livelihood. This article traces the role of many universities in India in support of this alternative system of education.

16.2 The Concept of Community College and its Salient Features

- The Community College is an alternative system of education, which is aimed at the empowerment of the disadvantaged and the underprivileged (Urban poor, Rural poor, Tribal poor and Women) through appropriate skills development leading to gainful employment in collaboration with the local industry and the community and achieve skills for employment and self employability of the above sections of people in the society.
- The Community College is an innovative educational alternative that is rooted in the Community providing holistic education and eligibility for employment to the disadvantaged.
- The Vision of the Community College is to be of the Community, for the Community and by the Community and to produce responsible citizens.
- The Community College promotes job oriented, work

related, skill - based and life coping education.

- The Community College initiative is in conformity with the Indian political will that prioritises in education, primary education, information technology education and vocational education.
- The key words of the Community College system are access, flexibility in curriculum and teaching methodology, cost effectiveness and equal opportunity in collaboration with industrial, commercial and service sectors of the local area and responding to the social needs and issues of the local community, internship and job placement within the local area, promotion of self employment and small business development, declaration of competence and eligibility for employment.

16.3 The Curriculum of a Community College

Category	Programme	Weeks	Hours	Credits
PART I	Life Skills	21 Weeks	630 Hours	21 Credits
PART II	Work Skills	21 Weeks	630 Hours	21 Credits
PART III	Internship and Hands on Experience	8 Weeks	390 Hours	13 Credits
PART IV	Preparation f or Employment and Evaluation	2 Weeks	60 Hours	2 Credits
TOTAL		52 Weeks	1710 Hours	57 Credits

- One Credit = 30 Hours of work.

16.4 Focus on Socio-Economic Weaker Sections (Target Group)

The Unique Achievement of the Community College has been the empowerment of the socially economically and educationally backward sections of society in the last 10 years. The Madras Centre has been able to gather the data regarding 30,101 from 122 Community Colleges. The breakup gives a complete picture of the Target Group Served.

Women - 76%
Married - 8%
Age - 16 – 48

Qualification

Below 10th - 19%; 10th Passed - 26%; 12th Passed - 47%; Degree- 08%

Caste

SC - 25%; ST - 07%; MBC - 16%; BC - 45%; OC - 09%

Monthly Family Income

Below 1000 - 38%; Below 2000 - 34%; Below 3000 - 17%; Above 3000 - 11%

Religion

Hindus - 54%; Christians - 43%; Muslims - 03%
Job Placement – 75%

16.5 Focus on Rural Development through Community Colleges

There is the urgent need to link Agriculture and Rural Development with Education for Livelihood and Skills Development. Due to the new emerging trends in Agricultural Farming and Rural Developmental Approaches to reach up to International standards, there is the need for the enhancement of Human Recourses and the developmental of newer and updating of skills. There is also the urgent necessity of harnessing the human resources and manpower of the Rural Community. This fits in well with the search of the Community College Movement.

(i) What is a Rural Community College?

Rural Community College has arisen as an urgent requirement for empowering the rural people through skills education for self-employment as well as group employment in rural areas.

(ii) The Features of Rural Community College

- Meets the needs of the local community
- People participating and people benefiting
- Aims at capacity building of rural people
- Improves talents of youth
- Taps resources and potentialities in rural areas.
- Provides skills for self-employment

- Creates job opportunities for eradicating poverty
- More field oriented with practical inputs
- Trains rural youth in traditional sectors.
- Enhances collaboration between government and service sector.
- Facilitates self-reliant initiatives in rural areas.
- Makes interested youth to upscale their education and skills
- Transforms the qualitative aspects of life of the rural poor
- Initiates sustainable livelihood options for poverty alleviation
- Empowers rural people through integrated development

(iii) Rationale for the Promotion of a Rural Community College

There is a great need for people, especially the young to discover great meaning and dignity in their lives and find positive, healthy, productive alternatives to unemployment, isolation, boredom, alienation, addiction and violence. Over 72% of the population in rural areas are not able to make a decent living mainly because of regular employment and income generation. Hence, creating gainful employment opportunities is the biggest challenge today.

The opportunities for regular employment and income generation in rural areas can be grouped into on-farm and off-farm activities. Initially, the agro-based activities cannot provide adequate opportunities for the landless laborers. But, subsequently, with the optimum use of resources and enhanced productivity, demand for labour will rise and even the landless will have increased employment opportunities with improvement in agriculture productivity, job opportunities for ancillary services will also increase and hereto, the landless laborers can take advantage of the situation. Based on the above rural development focus two community colleges have been started in Siruganur, Tamilnadu and Lachragarh, Jharkhand.

(iv) Lachragarh, Jharkhand

Montfort Community College is run by the Montfort Brothers of St. Gabriel, Ranchi Province. It is hoped that Montfort Community College would come up with a new educational system against the present system learning and give options to those who cannot progress in life due to poverty, weakness and injustice in the society. Therefore Community College aims at full development of those unemployed youth who cannot complete or cannot go to school. Community College will provide work efficiency to more youth every year which will give them much confidence to live prestigious life in the society and provide them the atmosphere for job opportunities. The institute will also provide them with a moral education and leadership programmes so as to form a good society.

Objectives

1. To provide skills and knowledge needed to cope with life's problems and challenges.
2. To develop a positive attitude
3. To understand the meaning of life and its challenges
4. To train to be successful and useful citizens through positive thinking.
5. To cope with criticism, failure, anger, loneliness, physical and verbal abuse
6. To manage time and stress.
7. To develop one's personality to its full potential.

Aims

1. To prevent labour migration especially thc migration of unskilled labours and migration of girls for working and maidservants.
2. Provide skill training, appropriate to make the youth get at least part time – employed.
3. Empower the powerless tribals and dalits.
4. Prevent the youth from becoming anti social elements and criminal and support them to become responsible citizens of the society.
5. Improve the economic status of tribals.

Courses Conducted by the Community College

1. Tailoring
2. Motor Mechanic
3. Carpentry
4. Welding
5. Masonry

(v) Ertram Rural Community College

Ertram Rural Community College is situated at the Human Resource Development Training Centre of VOICE Trust at Siruganur village in Mannachanallur Block, Trichy District, State of Tamilnadu, South India.

Siruganur is 25 Kilometers north of Trichy in the Trichy-Chennai National Highways (NH 45). It is linked by bus transportation between Trichy and Perambalur, the District Head Quarters of the neighbouring district of Perambalur at a distance of 30 kilometers north of Siruganur.

Siruganur is a village Panchayat of Mannachanallr block which has 156 villages big and small. It is one of the 38 village Panchayats of Mannachanallur Block.

Voice Trust (Voice for the Oppressed through Integrated Community Emancipation) was registered in 1985 under Trust act as a Non Profit and Voluntary Organisation. Being a NGO, VOICE Trust is involving in various social action initiatives for the disadvantaged groups of people especially, women, Children, Landless, Small Farmers, Unemployed Youth, The disabled, the Destitute and the Ageing.

Voice Trust obtained permission in 1986 from the Ministry of Home affairs, Government of India under the Foreign Contribution Regulation Act (FCRA)

Courses Conducted by the Community College

1. Diploma in Sustainable Farming Systems for Integrated Rural Development
2. Diploma in Pre- Primary Teacher Training
3. Diploma in House Electrician

4. Diploma in DTP Operator
5. Diploma in Plumbing Technology
6. Diploma in Fashion Designing and Garment Making

(vi) Village Placement Programme

President APJ Abdul Kalam has appreciated the Village Placement Programme of the Alagappa University and expressed the belief that such programmes would help the objectives of project achieved for Providing Urban Amenities to Rural Areas (PURA).

Kalam conveyed these views when Alagappa University Vice-Chancellor P. Kanniappan called on him at Rashtrapathi Bavan to brief the President of the Programme.

The Vice-Chancellor made mention of his meeting with the President at the feedback meeting on the university's innovative Village Placement Programme (VPP). He said that it was the first time that such a programme had been introduced by any university in the State. Over 400 students, both men and women, participated in the programme by staying in seven villages.

Students, who participated in the programme, told at the feedback meeting about their work in the villages, which included desilting village tanks.

(The New Indian Express, 13.10.2005)

16.6 Role of the Universities

• Tamil Nadu Open University helped the Community Colleges to receive recognition as Vocational Programme Centres.

1. ***Association with Tamil Nadu Open University***
   - The announcement in "The Hindu" dated 15.08.2004 "Job Oriented Programmes – The Tamil Nadu Open University (TNOU)" has introduced six job-oriented vocational programmes at the certificate level through the distance mode. In a statement here, the Vice-Chancellor, M.S. Palanichamy, said an intensive practical training to provide hands-on experience would be the mainstay of the programmes for DTP operator, house electrician, refrigeration

and air-conditioning technician, plumbing technician, four Wheeler mechanic and catering assistant. Community Colleges, Polytechnics, industrial training and other institutes with infrastructure would provide the practical inputs. Interested institutions may contact the Registrar, TNOU, Directorate of Technical Education Campus, Guindy, Chennai for obtaining forms and details within 15 days.

- Having seen the advertisement Dr. Xavier Alphonse, S.J., and the MCRDCE team approached Prof. M.S. Palanichamy, Vice Chancellor, Tamil Nadu Open University met him on the 17th of August 2004 and had a long discussion for about two hours about the possibility of offering above six courses in the Community Colleges.
- Dr. P. Thiyagarajan, Head, Continuing Education, TNOU was sent as a representative of the University as a one-man commission to visit Colleges in the city of Chennai. He visited Tabitha Community College, Vadapalani and Dr. Chandran Devanesan Rural Community College, Karanai Village on 20.08.2004. He was very much impressed by the functioning of Community College System. He was also happy to visit MCRDCE to get all the necessary information to know about the system.
- On 24.08.2004 Dr. Xavier Alphonse, S.J., made a presentation about the Community College system and its working at the Tamil Nadu Open University. The Members present were Prof. Palanichamy, Vice-Chancellor, Registrar, Dr. Thiyagarajan, Head, Continuing Education, Prof. Shanmugam, Consultant TNOU, Prof. Murugan, Director, Student Support Services, Prof. Subramanian, Continuing Education, Mr. Emmanuel, Manager, Dr. Chandran Devanesen Rural Community College, Mrs. Mercy Joy Joshua, Director, Chennai Corporation Community College, South Campus, Joseph Johnson, MCRDCE, Jothilingam, MCRDCE were present. We had a meeting of two hours at the end of which Vice-Chancellor requested Dr. Xavier Alphonse, S.J., to

have a consultation with Community Colleges in the State and also to arrange for a meeting of the Directors of Community Colleges with the whole team of Tamil Nadu Open University (TNOU).

Seventh Consultation of Community Colleges in Tamil Nadu

Accepting the invitation of the Vice-Chancellor, a consultation of Community Colleges in Tamil Nadu for recognition was organised and the dialogue with the TNOU Team on the *16th and 17th of September 2004* was conducted at Chennai.

The Purpose of the Seventh Consultation of Community Colleges

1. To familiarize with the working of the Tamil Nadu Open University especially with regard to the Six Vocational Courses.
2. To explore the feasibility of offering these six courses in our community colleges.
3. To request the university to accept the other popular courses that are run by the community colleges.
4. To have a dialogue with the TNOU about the modalities of offering the job-oriented courses.
5. To review and evaluate the functioning of the Community Colleges in Tamilnadu in terms of achievements, challenges and concerns.

About Tamil Nadu Open University

The Objectives

1. To provide an alternative non-formal, cost effective channel for obtaining tertiary education to those who seek it.
2. To supplement the efforts of Conventional University System in providing tertiary education thereby reducing the pressure on those systems.
3. To provide a "second chance" to those who had to discontinue their formal education for reasons of their own.
4. To provide easy access to good quality Higher Education to "all" in general and "the disadvantaged" in particular, by delivering the same at their door steps.

5. To provide an opportunity to those who are gainfully employed to upgrade their knowledge and skills tailored to meet specific vocational / professional needs, whenever they wish to do so.
6. To design an innovative system of good quality University Education that is flexible not only with respect to entry criteria, but also with respect to what to learn, when to learn and how to learn.
7. To design and provide local specific employment oriented programmes.

Prominent Features

TNOU has certain unique features such as:

1. State Jurisdiction
2. Flexible admission rules
3. Individualized study: flexibility, in terms of place, pace and duration of study
4. Use of latest information and communication technologies
5. Student support services network
6. Cost-effective programmes
7. Modular programmes
8. Resource sharing, collaboration and networking with other Open Universities
9. Relevant programmes

Based on the above Consultation *Tamil Nadu Open University (TNOU)* has recognised 79 Community Colleges in Tamil Nadu as Vocational Programme Centres. The recognition has also been extended to other Community Colleges in other parts of India. The following nine courses have been recognised as Diploma Courses to be conducted by Community Colleges from this year including Life Coping Skills and Communication Skills.

1. Pre School Teaching
2. Health Assistant
3. Fashion Design and Garment Making
4. DTP Operator

5. Refrigeration and Air Conditioning Technician
7. House Electrician
8. Plumbing Technician
8. Catering Assistant
9. Four Wheeler Mechanism

Advantages in going for the TNOU

- Formal Recognition
- Demand of the Target Group and the parents and the public
- Closer to the Community College System in philosophy, practice and implementation
- Diploma is valid all over India
- Possible for Registering in the Employment Exchanges of the country
- Possibility of taking care of the School dropouts since minimum qualification not prescribed except for Pre-Primary Teaching and Health Assistant Programmes
- Vocational Programme Centres
- Ensures status in the society
- Possibility of Vertical mobility through credit transfer since credits have been prescribed by the TNOU
- Scholarships (SC/ST and Common Wealth Scholarship) can be obtained through TNOU
  - Integration is useful to the Beneficiaries
  - Final Products have to be eligible for employment and should be able to meet with the demands of the required skills by the employers.
  - Broad spectrum of skills

2. *Yashwantrao Chavan Maharashtra Open University, Nashik*

MCRDCE Conducted a day's Consultation in Collaboration with Yashwantrao Chavan Maharashtra Open University at Nashik on 12th of August in which 66 participants took part from Maharashtra, Gujarat, Madhya Pradesh and Goa. The Vice Chancellor *Dr. Rajan M. Welukar* wanted by all means the

Community College system to be recognised by the Open University. The Proposals are being sent to the University for consideration

3. The Central University of Hyderabad

The MCRDCE Team was invited by the Central University of Hyderabad to speak to 60 participants of the Academic Staff College from all over India on the 2nd of November 2004. The Director of MCRDCE met the Vice–Chancellor, *Dr. Kota Harinarayana* who made a formal request to MCRDCE to help the rural youth in the neighbourhood. The University has started a Community College for the Rural Youth under the auspices of the Distance Education Centre with a course Industrial Security.

4. 1998 September

Establishment of *Five Community Colleges* by *Manonmaniam Sundaranar University* (M.S.University), Tirunelveli, Tamilnadu. It was further strengthened by starting of 36 Community Colleges during the years 1998-2005.

5. Avinashilingam Deemed University

Avinashilingam Deemed University is running a Community College for women from 1998.

6. Pondicherry Central University

This University started a Community College in October 1995 at the initiative of *Dr. Gnanam,* the then Vice –Chancellor of the Central University of Pondicherry. It is offering 5 Associate Degrees, 31 post graduate diplomas for those who have completed their degrees, One five year integrated course in M.A. Economics, 21 Diploma Courses for those who have completed +2, 18 certificate courses for those who have completed +2 and 10th standard with the duration of 2 months to 6 months. All these courses are conducted in close collaboration with the industries of the area. The college was inaugurated by the UGC Chairman Miss. Desai. As the prospectus of the college indicates, "Pondicherry University Community College endeavours to create an innovative alternative model of higher education in which academicians, administrators, industrialists, agriculturists, traders, students and other members of the community become partners in the development of human resource with adequate mutual collaboration and co-operation. In fact, the educational activities are designed in response to the needs of the local community, business, industries and Government. In other words, the community college is for the community and of the community and by the community.

7. *Madras University - Indian Community College System (ICCS) Document*

The Vice Chancellor, Dr. Thyagarajan of the University of Madras at the direction of the Chief Minister of Tamil Nadu constituted a working group to formulate a policy document of Indian Community College System (ICCS) in which Dr. Xavier Alphonse, was nominated as one of the six members. The document has been prepared with a clear idea of vertical mobility to bring in the Community College Students into the main stream of Higher Education non-credited courses, Diploma, Associate degree and degree.

16.7 University Grants Commission

The UGC proposed to introduce a scheme for institutionalising community colleges as a direct linkage to the conventional university/collegiate educational system. A report from the University of Madras on community colleges in Tamilnadu was received and a committee of experts would examine it and place it before the Union Human Recourse Development Ministry, Dr. Pillai said.

Under the scheme, the programmes conducted by the existing community colleges would be recognised by the higher education system. Madras University studied the community college – university linkage system in the United States.

The UGC studied the importance of community colleges run by non-governmental organisations. Governmental agencies in India, as also the successful experience in the U.S.Canada and other countries.

(The Hindu, March, 7, 2005)

16.8 Conclusion

It is very encouraging to note the involvement of the Universities in support of the Community College Movement in

India. The Community College System is gaining gradual acceptance because of the Universities coming forward to recognise and accept the system. The following suggestions can bring in a sea change in the whole scenario of the Higher Education in India.

- The four tier system of Higher Education non-credited, diploma, associate degree and degrees.
- Helping the Community College Students to have credit transfer to do the associate degree and degrees programmes.
- There is a need to develop new programmes through Distance Education Centres of various Universities to suit the learning needs and enhancement and updating of skills of the Community College students.

It is very promising if all these suggestions could be implemented, the takers of Higher Education will increase from 7% to 20% in India and 13% would be definitely from the socio economic weaker sections of the society.

17

Directory of the Community Colleges and the Courses Given

17.1 Non-Governmental Organisations Community Colleges – 62

1. Madras Community College, Chennai; *(October, 1995)*
2. Madurai Community College, Madurai; *(August, 1996)*
3. Melapudur St.Anne's Community College, Trichy; *(July, 1998)*
4. Immaculate Community College, Cuddalore; *(September, 1998)*
5. Periyakulam St. Anne's Community College, Periyakulam; *(September, 1998)*
6. Chennai Corporation Community College, Chennai; *(Feb, 1999)*
7. Kuthenkuly Community College, Kuthenkuly; *(July, 1999)*
8. Amala Annai Rural Community College, Devakottai; *(August, 1999)*
9. Dharmapuri RIDO Rural Community College, Dharmapuri Dt., *(August, 1999)*
10. Dindigul Community College, Dindigul; (August, 1999)
11. Sadhana Rural Community College, Madurai; *(August, 2000)*
12. Kothagiri Community College, Kothagiri; *(September, 2000)*

13. RUHSA Community College, Vellore Dt.; *(October, 2000)*
14. Devaki Community College, Karaikudi; *(July, 2001)*
15. 21st Century International Community College, Sivagangai; *(July, 2001)*
16. Udhayam Rural Community College for Women, Thuraiyur; *(August, 2001)*
17. Nirmala Community College, Chennai; *(August, 2001)*
18. Baba Community College, Sivagangai Dt; *(August, 2001)*
19. Jeyaprakash Narayan Community College, Porur, Chennai; *(December, 2001)*
20. Chrompet Community College, Chrompet, Chennai;*(February, 2002)*
21. Kancheepuram Community College, *(June, 2002)*
22. Ertram Rural Community College, Trichy Dt., *(April, 2002)*
23. Adaikala Annai Community College, Pallavaram *(July, 2002)*
24. Tabitha Community College, Vadapalani; *(July, 2002)*
25. Dr. Chandran Devanesen Rural Community College, Navallur Post; *(July, 2002)*
26. Sahaya Annai Community College, Madurai; *(July, 2002)*
27. YWCA Community College, Chennai; *(August, 2002)*
28. Nano Nagle Community College, Chennai; *(August, 2002)*
29. Sivagangai Community College, Sivagangai; *(August, 2002)*
30. SEVAI Community College, Allur, Trichy Dt.; *(August, 2002)*
31. Notre Dame Community College, Colachel, Kanyakumari Dt.; *(June, 2003)*
32. Loyola Community College, Ranipet; *(July, 2003)*
33. Don Bosco Community College, Dindigul; *(July, 2003)*
34. Smile Community College, Kalaiyarkovil; *(July, 2003)*

35. Tabitha Community College, Kellys, Chennai; *(August, 2003)*
36. Tabitha Community College, Aminjikarai, Chennai; *(August, 2003)*
37. St. Arulanandar Community College, Kuppayanallur; *(September, 2003)*
38. Sacred Heart Community College, Villupuram; *(October, 2003)*
39. Pravaham Community College, Vellore Dt.; *(February, 2004)*
40. Poorani Community College, Karaikudi; *(July, 2004)*
41. Stanisma Community College, Sivagangai; *(July, 2004)*
42. Timothy Community College, Kottivakam, Chennai; *(August, 2004)*
43. Loyola Community College, Kilpennathur; *(December, 2004)*
44. St. Anne's Community College, Aralvaimozhy, Kanyakumari Dt.; *(March, 2005)*
45. Zen Community College, Karaikudi; *(May, 2005)*
46. Jeevan Rural Community College, Srivillipudur; *(June, 2005)*
47. Coonoor Community College, Nilgiris Dt.; *(July, 2005)*
48. St. Charles Community College, Jolarpet; *(July, 2005)*
49. Karunakarya Community College, Chennai; *(July, 2005)*
50. Joan of Arc Community College, Mannarpuram, Tirunelveli Dt., *(July, 2005)*
51. IID Tabor Community College, Mamallapuram; *(July, 2005)*
52. Trichy Community College, Trichy; *(July, 2005)*
53. Nagle Community College, Theni Dt.; *(July, 2005)*
54. Jasper Daniel Community College, Mathuravoyal, Chennai; *(August, 2005)*

55. Bharat Community College, Chennai; *(August, 2005)*
56. Veda Mari Community College, Villupuram Dt.; *(August, 2005)*
57. St. Patrick's Community College, Villupuram Dt.; *(September, 2005)*
58. Arcot Lutheran Church Community College, Cuddalore; *(September, 2005)*
59. St. Joseph's Community College, Nagapatinam; *(September, 2005)*
60. Kaaniyappa Community College, Arani, Thiruvallur Dt.; *(September, 2005)*
61. Holy Cross Community College, Kulasekaram; *(September, 2005)*
62. Kovalam Community College, Kancheepuram Dt.; *(November, 2005)*

M.S. University Community Colleges – 34

Tirunelveli Region

63. Palayamkottai Community College, Tirunelveli; *(September, 1998)*
64. SCAD Community College, Cheranmahadevi, Tirunelveli; *(September, 1998)*
65. Sardar Raja Community College, Vadakangulam; *(September, 1998)*
66. Asir Community College, Tirunelveli Dist.; *(July, 1999)*
67. St. Luke's Community College, Nazareth, Tuticorin Dist; *(July, 1999)*
68. Sri. P. Pitchandi Memorial Community College, Tuticorin; *(July, 1999)*
69. Barenbruck Community College, Surandai, Tirunelveli Dt.; *(July, 1999)*
70. Sundaram Arul Raj Community College, Tuticorin; *(July, 1999)*
71. C.K.T. Community College, Ettayapuram; *(July, 1999)*

72. Bishop Selwyn Community College, Palayamkottai; *(July, 1999)*
73. Sr. Nivedita Community College, Ariyakulam, Tirunelveli; *(July, 1999)*
74. Nanguneri Rural Community College, Tirunelveli; *(July, 1999)*
75. Yamini Amma Community College, Vilattikulam; *(July, 2000)*
76. Athithya Community College, Tenkasi;*(July, 2000)*
77. RVS Community College, Tirunelveli Dt.; *(July, 2000)*
78. P.S. Community College, Tirunelveli Dt.; *(July, 2002)*
79. Spectrum Community College, Tirunelveli; *(July, 2003)*
80. Trust Community College, Tirunelveli Dt.; *(July, 2005)*

Nagercoil Region

81. Noorul Islam Community College, Kumarakoil; *(September, 1998)*
82. St. Mary's Community College, Kanyakumari Dist; *(July, 1999)*
83. Kanyakumari Community College, Kanyakumari; *(July, 1999)*
84. Mulagumoodu Vicariate Community College, Mulagumoodu; *(July, 2000)*
85. MET Community College, Kanyakumari Dt.; *(July, 2000)*
86. Ramachandra Community College, Kanyakumari Dt.; *(July, 2000)*
87. Good Shepherd Community College, Nagercoil ; *(July, 2000)*
88. Grace Community College, Kaliakkavilai; *(July, 2000)*
89. Bensam Community College, Nagercoil; *(July, 2000)*
90. CSI- Bellpin Community College, Tirunelveli; *(July, 2002)*

91. Vivekananda Community College, Agastheeswaram; *(July, 2000)*

92. Mary Jenkins Memorial Community College, Kanyakumari; *(July, 2003)*

93. Rajendra Community College, Kanyakumari; *(July, 2003)*

94. Jeyachandra Community College, Kanyakumari Dt.; *(July, 2004)*

95. Zion Community College, Nagercoil; *(July, 2004)*

96. C.N. Community College, Nagercoil; *(July, 2004)*

University Community Colleges -2

97. Avinashilingam University Community College, Coimbatore; *(July, 1998)*

98. Bharathidasan University Community College, Trichy; *(December, 1998)*

PONDICHERRY

University Community College -01

99. Pondicherry University Community College; *(June, 1995)*

Non-Governmental Organisations Community College - 01

100. Karaikal Community College, CEDA Trust, Karaikal; *(July, 2005)*

101. IID Tabor Community College, Karaikal; *(July, 2005)*

ANDHRA PRADESH

Non-Governmental Organisations Community College - 06

102. Tenali JMJ Community College, Tenali; *(July, 1999)*

103. JMJ Community College, Hanuman Junction; *(July, 1999)*

104. Asakiranam Community College, Eluru; *(January, 2003)*

105. St. Joseph's Community College, Visakhapatnam; *(August, 2005)*

106. St.Ann's Community College, Arilova, Visakhapatnam; *(August, 2005)*

107. St.Ann's Community College, Rajam, Srikakulam Dt.; *(August, 2005)*

University Community College – 01

108. University of Hyderabad Community College, Hyderabad; *(September, 2005)*

KARNATAKA

109. Bannerghatta Community College, Bangalore; *(August, 2001)*

110. K.G.F. Community College, Kolar Gold Fields; *(August, 2001)*

111. Tarbes Community College, Bangalore; *(March, 2003)*

112. St. Xavier's Community College, Khanapur, Belgaum; *(July, 2003)*

113. St. Teresa's Community College, Mysore; *(August, 2003)*

114. Angels Community College, Bangalore; *(September, 2004)*

115. Ashirvad Community College, Bangalore; *(July, 2005)*

116. Bangalore Community College, Bangalore; *(July, 2005)*

117. Gulbarga Community College, Gulbarga; *(July, 2005)*

118. Our Lady of Victories Community College, KGF; *(August, 2005)*

119. Adarsha Foundation Community College, Bangalore; *(August, 2005)*

KERALA

120. Auxilium Community College, Kottiyam; *(September, 2001)*

121. Vikasini Community College, Cochin; *(August, 2001)*

122. Auxilium Community College, Kattappana; *(July, 2002)*

123. Auxilium Community College, Palluruthy; *(July, 2002)*

124. Kitex Community College, Aluva, Cochin; *(December, 2002)*
125. Auxilium Community College, Trivandrum; *(July, 2003)*
126. Teresian Community College, Kalamassery, Cochin; *(November, 2003)*
127. T.K.M. Community College, Kollam; *(December, 2003)*
128. Archbishop Powathil Assumption Community College, Kottayam; *(July, 2005)*

MAHARASHTRA

129. Vivekananda Community College, Jalgaon; *(July, 2001)*
130. Auxilium Community College, Ahmednagar; *(June, 2004)*

MADHYA PRADESH

131. Bhopal Community College, Bhopal; *(July, 2004)*
132. St. Aloysius Community College (St. Aloysius College Campus); *(July, 2004)*
133. St. Aloysius Community College, (JOGNI Campus); *(July, 2004)*
134. St. Aloysius Community College, (Satyalayam Campus); *(July, 2004)*

GUJARAT

135. Vidhyadeep Community College, Bharuch; *(July, 1999)*
136. Rtn. Kalyan Banerjee Rofel Community College, Vapi; *(July, 2002)*

GOA

137. St. Xavier's Community College, Mapusa; *(August, 2003)*

UTTARANCHAL

138. Seventh Day Adventist Community College, Roorkee; *(January, 2001)*

JHARKHAND

139. AID Community College, Garhwa; *(July, 2001)*
140. Montfort Community College, Lachragarh, Simdega Dt.; *(December, 2003)*

141. Ursuline Community College, Noatoli, Gumla Dt.; *(February, 2004)*
142. Montfort Community College, Noatoli, Gumla Dt.; *(June, 2004)*
143. St. Joseph's Community College, Simdega Dt.; *(December, 2004)*
144. Montfort Community College, Hazaribagh; *(March, 2005)*
145. Deepanjali Community College, Gumla; *(November, 2005)*

DELHI

146. Lokabodhan Community College, New Delhi; *(August, 2001)*

CHHATTISGARH

147. Kerakacchar Community College, Pathalgaon; *(September, 2002)*
148. Bhainswar Community College, Korea Dt.; *(September, 2002)*
149. Rajpur Community College, Chhattisgarh; *(September, 2002)*

ORISSA

150. UPAYA Science and Technology Community College, Rajgangpur; *(May, 2005)*

HIMACHAL PRADESH

151. M.S. Panwar Community College, Solan; *(May, 2005)*

HARYANA

152. CSST Community College, Faridabdad; *(August, 2005)*

WEST BENGAL

153. Cluny Community College, Kalimpong; *(August, 2005)*

KARNATAKA

154. Rosa Mystica Community College, Managalore; *(January, 2006)*

17.2 Courses Conducted in the Community Colleges in India

S.No	The Name of the Course	No.of Community Colleges
1.	Health Assistant	92
2.	DTP Operator	66
3.	Pre Primary Teacher Training	65
4.	Fashion Designing and Garment Making	47
5.	Refrigeration and Air Conditioning Technician	17
6.	House Electrician	28
7.	Catering Assistant / Hotel Management	16
8.	Four Wheeler Mechanism	19
9.	Plumbing Technology	8
10.	Tally Accounting	2
11.	Beautician / Beauty Culture	3
12.	Medical Lab Technology	7
13.	Office Secretary / Secretarial Practice	29
14.	Computer Hardware	6
15.	Two Wheeler Mechanism	8
16.	Cargo Management	3
17.	Sales / Marketing Management	3
18.	Travel Management	5
19.	Bakery and Confectionery	2
20.	Printing Technology / Printing	5
21.	Camera Operating	1
22.	Naattu Vaidhyam	2
23.	Rural Marketing	1
24.	Communtiy Enterprises	1
25.	Heritage Tourism	1
26.	Rural Service	1
27.	Community Development Worker	1
28.	Typing	1
29.	Food Processing / Food Preservation	3
30.	Medical Radiography	2
31.	Physiotheraphy	1
32.	Leather Technology	1
33.	Information Technology	1
34.	Agricultural Farming	1
35.	Small Business Management	2
36.	Vermi Composting	1
37.	Fitter	4
38.	Veterinary Health Assistant	4
39.	House Keeping	2
40.	Business Account / Chatered Account	2
41.	Yoga and Health Science	1
42.	Carpentry	3
43.	Welding	6
44.	Masonry	3
45.	Radio and Television Mechanism	1
46.	Orchids and Anthurium Cultivation	1

18

The Mission of the Community Colleges

18.1 Target Group Served

The Unique Achievement of the Community Colleges has been the empowerment of the socially, economically and educationally backward sections of society in the last 10 years. The Madras Centre has been able to gather the data regarding 30,101 from 122 Community Colleges. The breakup gives a complete picture of the Target Group Served. Women - 76%, Married - 8%, Age - 16 – 48, Qualification Below 10th - 19%; 10th Passed - 26%; 12th Passed -47%; Degree- 08%, Caste, SC - 25%; ST- 07%; MBC - 16%; BC - 45%; OC - 9%, Monthly Family Income - Below 1000 - 38%; Below 2000 - 34%; Below 3000 - 17%; Above 3000 - 11%, Religion - Hindus - 54%; Christians - 43%; Muslims - 03% Job Placement – 75%. Thus the concept is totally a secular one breaking all barriers of religion, caste, region, language and educational qualification.

Profile of 30,101 Community College Students from 122 Community Colleges

1. Total No: of Students

Year	*Total No. of Students*
1996 – 1997	174
1997 – 1998	204
1998 – 1999	577
1999 – 2000	1,815
2000 – 2001	2,282
2001 – 2002	2,933

2002 – 2003	3,840
2003 – 2004	4,815
2004 – 2005	6,969
2005 – 2006	6,492
Total	**30,101**

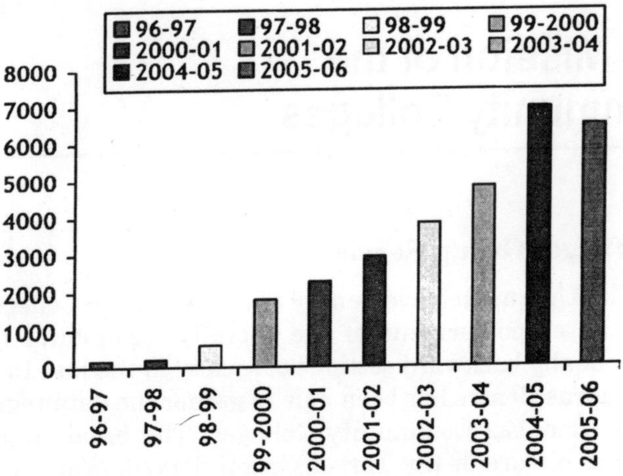

2. Male / Female (122 Community Colleges)

Male	– 7,098
Female	– 23,003
Total	**– 30,101**

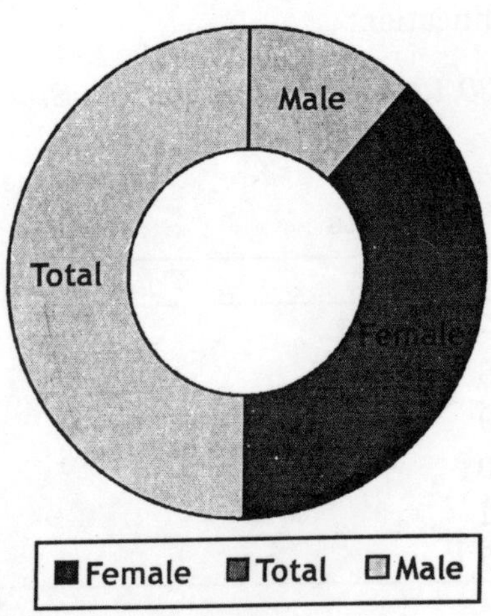

3. Married / Unmarried (122 Community Colleges)

Married	–	2,387
Unmarried	–	27,714
Total	-	**30,101**

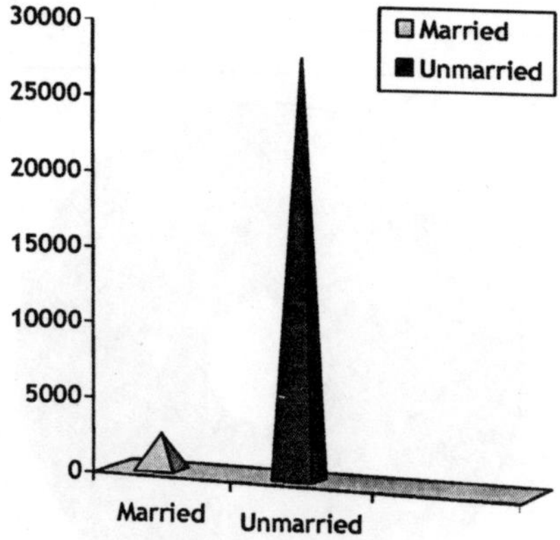

4. Age (122 Community Colleges)

16-18	-	10,640
19-21	-	13,009
22-25	-	3,851
26-30	-	1,571
31-34	-	714
35–above	-	316
Total	-	**30,101**

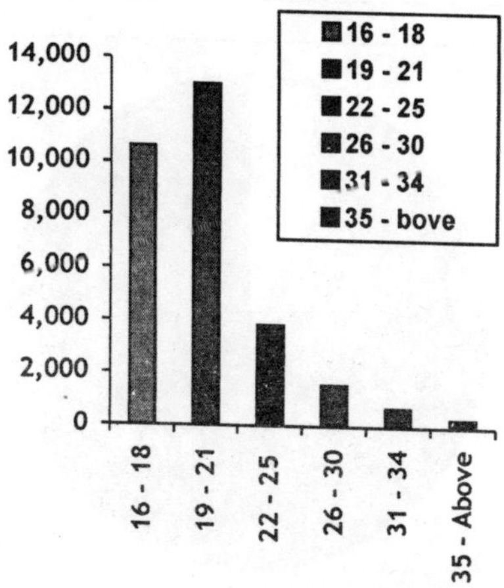

5. Qualification (122 Community Colleges)

Below 10th	-	5,930
10th Passed	-	7,669
12th Passed	-	14,142
Degree	-	2,333
Total	-	**30,101**

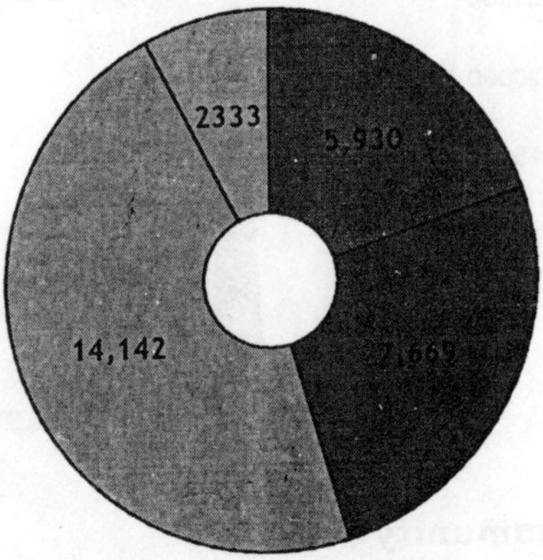

6. Caste (122 Community Colleges)

SC	-	7,602
ST	-	2,097
MBC	-	4,758
BC	-	12,847
OC	-	2,797
Total	-	**30,101**

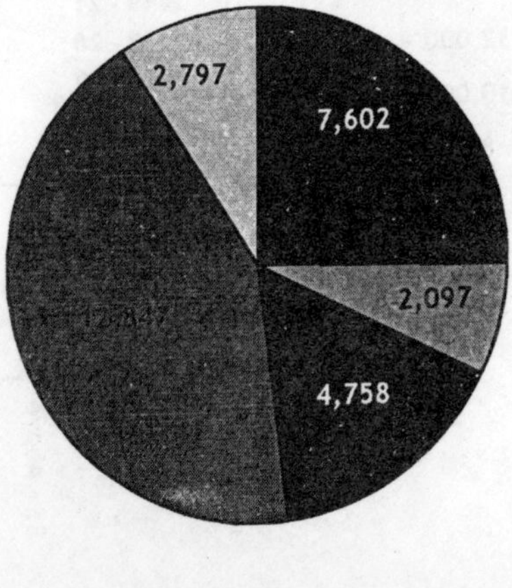

7. Monthly Family Income (122 Community Colleges)

Below Rs.1,000	-	11,437
Rs.1,001 – Rs.2,000	-	10,376
Rs.2,001 – Rs.3,000	-	5,084
Rs.3,001 – above	-	3,204
Total	-	**30,101**

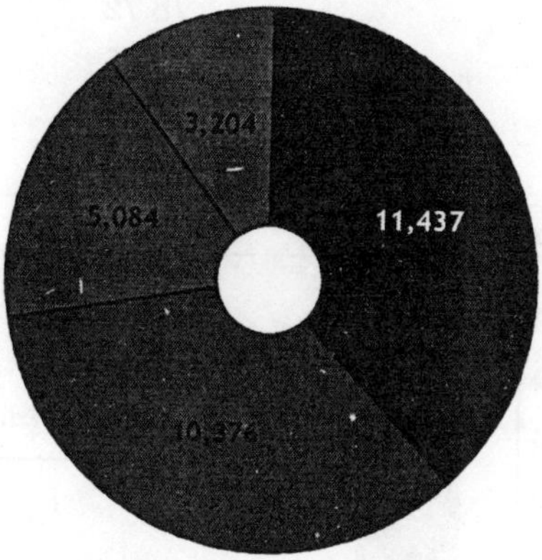

8. Religions (122 Community Colleges)

Hindus	-	16,252
Christian	-	12,981
Muslims	-	868
Total	-	**30,101**

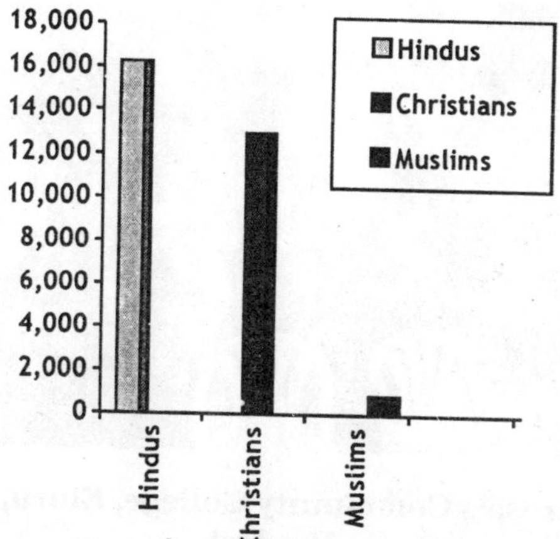

9. Job Placements

Year	Job Placement%	Hr.Edu%
1997-1998	81.26	09.37
1998-1999	75.04	22.49
1999-2000	66.26	20.49
2000-2001	72.84	15.16
2001-2002	78.72	16.14
2002-2003	74.75	12.19
2003-2004	76.54	12.61
2004-2005	71.12	15.79
TOTAL Average	**74.57**	**15.53**

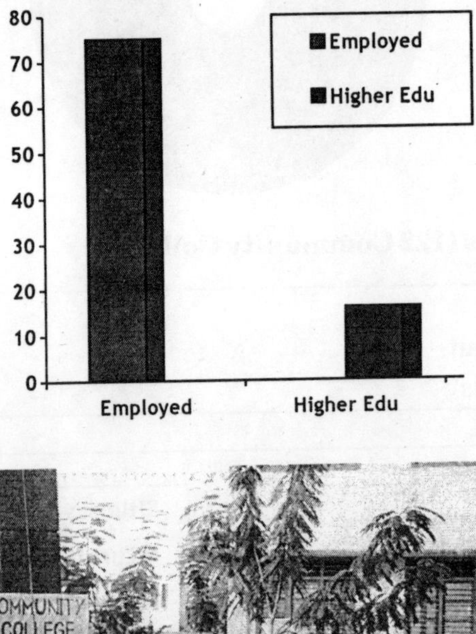

St. Theresa's Community College, Eluru, Andhra Pradesh

Kitex Community College, Aluva, Kerala

Vidhyadeep Community College, Bharuch, Gujarat

Ursuline Community College, Noatoli, Jharkhand

Madurai Community College, Tamil Nadu

Tarbes Community College, Bangalore, Karnataka

Auxilium Community College, Kottiyam, Kerala

Dr. Chandran Devanesan Rural Community College, Karanai Village, Tamil Nadu

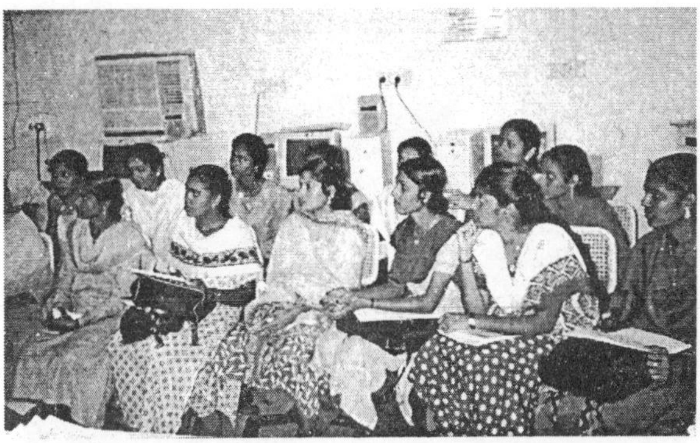

Chennai Corporation Community College, (South Campus), Tamilnadu

Teresian Community College, Kalamaserry, Kerala

Nano Nagle Community College, Chennai, Tamilnadu

KGF Community College, KGF, Karnataka

Montfort Rural Community College, Lachragarh, Jharkhand

Auxilium Community College, Kottiyam, Kerala

18.2 The Success Stories of the Community College Students

The students who have gone through Community Colleges have gone though transformation in their lives.

R. Vanitha *(Beautician and health care) – Dr. Chandran Devanesen Community College, Karanai Village.*

A married woman who has two small children and her husband was stabbed to death by the people who lent him money. Having discontinued the 10th standard, she did not know as to

how to battle with life. Because of her performance and attitude, she was absorbed by the beauty parlour, which trained her on the above work skill. She is now completely taking care of the parlor, educating her kids and set aside a remarriage proposal made by her parents.

T. Saravana Kumar *(Two wheeler mechanic) –Dr. Chandran Devanesen Community College, Karanai Village.*

A 10th standard failed boy, has no father but has an aged mother lived on the support of his married sister, to whom he was giving all his earning got by doing painting and white washing

before joining the community college. After having joined the college, he couldn't support the family, so he suffered mentally and physically. Even then, he attended the college. Sometimes he used to go to bus depot to wash the vehicles in the nighttime. Many times he tried to dropout from the college and somehow he was able to complete the course. After completing the community college education, instead of finding a job based on the work skills training, he got a job in a Xerox and STD booth for Rs. 1500 per month. Gradually he explored all the viable means to earn more money. Now he has got a dealership for Arokia milk and runs three STD booths on lease. His monthly income is approximately Rs. 20,000 per month and has employed 12 boys and girls of whom some of them are doing graduation.

Ms. R. Sirumalar *(Office Management) – Madurai Community College.*

R. Sirumalar studied in the year 1997-98. After completing her X standard, due to her poor economic family background,

she was unable to continue her studies. Her relatives helped her to join MCC and she was provided fee concession for her studies. After completing her diploma in Madurai Community College, she joined the Susee Auto, Madurai as Office Assistant, now working in Susee Auto, Rajapalayam as Computer Operator and earning Rs.7, 000 per month.

Ms. Padma Tadvi (Secretarial Course) – Vidhyadeep Community College, Bharuch, Gujarat.

Padma comes from a background village in the Panchmahal district of Gujarat, where women are not encouraged at all for

education. The sisters recommended her to do the Secretarial course at Vidhyadeep Community College and sponsored her education for two years.

Padma showed leadership qualities during her studies at Vidhyadeep. She joined the course in 2002 and completed it successfully in 2004, having secured a scholarship after the first year itself and a prize in the second year.

In April 2004, soon after completing her Secretarial course, Padma found a job. She worked there for some time and then shifted to another job which would get her a better salary. In June 2004, she was offered a good job in Baroda in an organization which trains students in English and prepares them to migrate to Canada. She speaks English well and is working at Vyaktitva in Baroda. Her immediate plan is to join the University and register for B.Com. Her boss, seeing her talents, encouraged her to improve her educational qualifications, so that she can improve her prospects.

Ms. Nitaben Kantubhai Gamit (Nursing Assistant), Vidhyadeep Community College, Bharuch, Gujarat.

Nitaben comes from a poor family in a remote village called Varjakhan in Surat District. Both her parents are labourers and

work in the fields of others. They also earn a living by rearing goats. Nita has a married sister and a grand mother who lives with her family.

After Std XII Nita joined Vidhyadeep Community College and got admission for the Nursing Assistant's Course. She took active interest in all the activities of the course and enjoyed. Her great desire was to be a good nurse and to serve the poor. For her training placement, she was sent to the Paraspada centre of Dharampur mission where she worked for 6 weeks. Here is the feedback given by Sr. Nita who was in charge of that mission.

"Thank you very much for sending Nitaben to Dharampur mission (Paraspada) for her practical experience. She has been a great help to us. She was ready to do any work such as helping in the dispensary, giving classes to the health workers, conducting meetings for the mahila mandal ladies and seeing to the various needs of the boarders.

She has a very pleasant nature. She is hardworking, responsible, reliable and sociable. She took interest in the dispensary to learn things. If she continues like this she can prove to be a smart nurse".

Ms. Rani, Auxilium Community College, Trivandrum, Kerala.

Ms. Rani, after attending Life Coping Skills class, I could accept myself. Through this I feel that my friends also accept me. If anybody points my mistakes I accept it and try to correct them.

When I take charge of any duty I will do it perfectly. I have a clear responsibility in it. I am thinking about the facts and the person positively. I had a fear that what other people think about me. But now I know I am in the safe hands of the heavenly father. Now I am not giving much importance to my defects. I understood that I have many good qualities.

Mrs.Mariam Kishori Minj (Tailoring and Embroidery), Ursuline Community College, Noatoli, Jharkhand.

My name is *Mariam Kishori Minj.* I am B.A., B.Ed., I have no job. I am qualified therefore I did not like to be just a house

wife. I feel useless alone remaining at home. I was feeling aimless. I have the great desire to learn tailoring, embroidery and other skills available in Ursuline Community College Noatoli.

The life coping skills changed my life. I got self confidence and hope in my life. Now I feel that I can be a social worker. I will work for the poor. I am happy to share my life with you.

Mr. S. Jothibasu (Radio and TV Mechanism), RUHSA Community College, Vellore Dt., Tamil Nadu.

Mr. S. Jothibasu completed his Radio and TV Mechanism (1991-1992). He belongs to Backward Class and his monthly family income is Rs. 5,000. He passed his Tenth Standard and joined the Community College. He learnt Life coping Skills, coping with failure. At internship, he gained experience in customer satisfaction and good relationship with the owner. At present, he is working at Gudiyatham and he is earning of *Rs. 5,000.*

Mr. N. Sudakar (Automobile and four-wheeler mechanism), RUHSA Community College, Vellore Dt., Tamil Nadu.

Mr. N. Sudakar completed his Automobile and four-wheeler mechanism (1999-2000). He belongs to backward class and his monthly family income is Rs. 5,000. He completed his Tenth Standard and joined Community College. At his internship, he gained experience in repairing the vehicle. At present he is having his own workshop and earning a monthly salary of *Rs. 5,000.*

Mr. E. Paulsamy (Computer Application), SCAD Community College, Tirunelveli, Tamil Nadu.

Mr. E. Paulsamy completed his DCA Course (1999-2000). He belongs to Most Backward class. His monthly family income is Rs. 1,200. He finished his plus two at a private school. While doing his course in Community College, he knows how to develop positive attitude, to cope with stress and to set his goals. He has improved his communication skills and good relationship with others. At present, he is working in Evergreen Marketers, Coimbatore and earning a monthly salary of *Rs. 2,500.*

D. Sathish Kumar (Hotel Management), Chennai Corporation Community College (South Campus), Tamil Nadu.

Mr. D. Sathish Kumar completed his Hotel Management. He belongs to SC caste and his monthly family income is Rs. 3,000. He discontinued his Batchelor's degree and joined the Community College. He knows how to achieve goals. At internship, he gained experience and knowledge of preparing Vegetarian and Non-Vegetarian Dishes. At present, he is working at Hotel Savera, Chennai and earning a monthly salary of *Rs. 3,200.*

M. Arokya Das (Office Secretaryship), RIDO Community College, Dharmapuri, Tamil Nadu.

Mr. M. Arokya Das completed his Office Secretary (1999-2000). He belongs to Backward class family. His educational qualification was B.A. His monthly family income is Rs.560. After joining the community college, he learned to cope with life, During the internship he got the experience of maintaining the record, to know the office functioning. At present, he is working at Aravind eye hospital and earning a Salary of *Rs. 6,000.*

B. Meganathan (Four Wheeler Mechanism and Driving), RIDO Community College, Dharmapuri, Tamil Nadu.

Mr. B. Meganathan completed his four-wheeler mechanism and driving (2000-2001). He completed his tenth standard. He belongs to the backward class and his monthly family income is Rs.1,400. After joining the community college, he was able to understand problems of others and feelings. During internship, he gained experience in maintaining the vehicle, problems with the machine. He is self employed and earning *Rs.5,000.*

M. Periyasamy (Electrical and Electronics), Nanguneri Rural Community College, Tamil Nadu.

Mr. M. Periyasamy completed his Electrical and Electronic Course (1999-2000). He belongs to SC Caste and his monthly family income is Rs. 2,400. He joined the Community College and gained knowledge in Personality Development and Communication Skills. During his internship he gained experience in his work. At present, he is working at Eureka Forbes Ltd., and earning a monthly salary of *Rs. 4,000.*

19

Indian Community College System

19.1 Background

In view of the fact that the University of Madras is accorded the status of *"University with Potential for Excellence"* by the University Grants Commission, the mandate of the University in higher education has unfolded to international dimension. It has further becomes obligatory for our University to innovate in higher education since the university is one of the three first formed Universities in modern India in the year 1857 and is going to celebrate Her 150th year by 2006-07.

International Higher Education has more recently provided another avenue of *'reaching the unreached youth'* by a para-formal mode of higher education in addition to the existing formal college mediated-regular education and the non-formal distance-mode education. It is shown in the United States of America and Germany that the American Community College system and the German Industrial School system have emerged as the successful para-formal mode of higher education. They cater to the *"missing link"* by providing aptitude based flexible entrepreneurial education for the youth who could not acquire regular formal education and also address the present day *"mismatch"* between the existing higher education products and the requirements of the job market by their continuing education to every one.

India is indeed in an important juncture of 'educational vibrancy' to bring about 100% literacy through its *'Sarva Shiksha Abhiyan'* scheme on one hand and to enhance higher education rate to the eligible youth from the existing 7% to about 20% in the next one decade. Since the existing formal and non-formal modes of Indian higher education systems may not be able to fully satisfy the aspirations of the youth and requirements of the country, the University of Madras has conceptualised a para-formal mode of higher education which is culturally appropriate to our country and christened it as *"Indian Community College System"*.

With the appreciation and approval of this concept by Honourable Chief Minister of Tamil Nadu, Selvi J. Jayalalithaa during my meeting on 8th September 2004 and as requisitioned by Honourable Madam for a full fledge proposal document, the University of Madras constituted the following Committee of Experts to discuss, design and formulate the document.

Chairperson

Prof. S.P. Thyagarajan
Vice-Chancellor, University of Madras

Member Secretary

Prof. K.S. Raghavan
Dean-Academic, University of Madras

Members

1. Mr. Ravi S. Candadai,
   Consul for Public Affairs,
   Consulate of the United States of America, Chennai
   [Formerly associated with American Community College in USA]
2. Fr. Dr. Xavier Alphonse, S.J.
   Director,
   Madras Centre for Research and Development of Community
   Education, Chennai-600 028
   [Originator for Community College in Tamil Nadu]
3. Commissioner of Technical Education,
   Directorate of Technical Education, Government of Tamil Nadu
   [Agency Implementing Community Polytechniques in Tamil Nadu]

4. Mr. L. Jayachandran,
Assistant Director [SPCU-CICP]
Directorate of Technical Education, Government of Tamil Nadu
[Implementing Indo-Canadian Project on Community Polytechniques in Tamil Nadu]
5. Dr. C.N. Natarajan
Special Officer for Community College
Manonmaniam Sundaranar University, Tirunelveli
6. Dr. K. Parthasarathy
Director, Center for Adult, Continuing Education and Extension
Bharathidasan University, Tiruchirapalli

In addition to indepth deliberations, an Indo-US Workshop on "Community College System" was organised by the University of Madras on 8th February 2005 in Collaboration with the US Consulate at Chennai. Dr. Robert Templin, President, North Virginia Community College, USA, Vice-Chancellors of the Universities in Tamil Nadu, experts in higher education from India and USA and the representative of the existing community colleges in India participated and provided inputs.

The final document as approved by the Expert Committee is being presented to Honourable Chief Minister of Tamil Nadu with the request to consider this document for adoption by Government of Tamil Nadu and also for recommending it to University Grants Commission and Government of India for consideration as a para-formal mode of higher education to the country as a whole.

[S.P. Thyagarajan]
Vice-Chancellor
University of Madras

19.2 Framework for and Indian Commnity College System

1. Definition

A Community College is a comprehensive institution of higher education offering education offering educational programme at post-secondary school level which generally include, but are not limited to courses in occupation and technical fields and continuing education to meet the workforce needs of the region in which the college is located and also offering 'bridge' programme to serve as a 'link' to mainstream higher education.

1.1 Need for Indian Community College System (ICCS): The need for a parallel system of community college education arises largely from the limitation of the existing system of education in meeting the present and emerging needs for workforce and the gaps obtaining therein:

- The present system is unable to cater to the higher education needs of large segment of our society. It has been estimated that only 7% of the qualified people in the relevant age group enter higher education system. In the emerging economy, access to post-secondary education has become the threshold requirement for success of individuals. We should aim at achieving access to higher education for at least 20% of the eligible youth
- The *PURA* (Providing Urban Amenities to Rural Areas) concept of His Excellency, the President of India requires that we establish appropriate mechanism for providing opportunities in terms of access to education, gainful employment and encouraging entrepreneurship among rural youth
- The school drop out rate for the age group 11-17 years in India is a huge 50%+
- There appears to be a 'mismatch' between the preset system of higher education and the requirements of job market. Globalization and market driven needs require that the "right type" of vocational and entrepreneurial education is provided to ensure the availability of the required workforce; the country's employment exchanges indicate that there are over 40 million people registered at the employment exchanges seeking job positions, 70% of whom are educated. While large segments of our educated remain unemployment or underemployment, there are emerging job positions (at lower and middle levels) for which suitably equipped personnel are not available. Careers in health care, office management, medical records transcription, technical writing, advertising, teaching automobile industry,

hospitality industry, printing and publishing industry, construction industry, call centres are a few such areas. Indeed many of these careers focus on job requirement that are characterized by a very rapid product cyberspace, automation, business processes out-sourcing and a work place that has generally adopted a much higher degree of sophistication than ever before. This suggests that there are gaps in the pattern of vocational education system prevalent in the country which has inadvertently given a hope of white-collared employment. Hence there is a need for ensuring a system of value-added education with programmes designed to meet the needs of the job market and society.

- The need for continuing education of professionals and displaced workers in new skills is increasingly being felt.
- It has often been remarked that the Indian system of education trains excellent professionals but only a few entrepreneurs! In a country with a large population, it is important also to train people equipped with entrepreneurial skills, especially for setting up small businesses and trades so that the younger people get trained not only as skill built employees but also as capacity built employers.
- The need for a system that will address the educational aspirations of the beneficiaries of the *Sarva Shiksha Abhiyan* will be increasing felt in the coming years.

2. Mission

In view of the above the single most important philosophy that underpins community colleges is *'Provision of Universal access to higher education'*. The mission of a community college is to provide relevant, affordable, Flexible and accessible post-secondary educational programmes with a slant to vocational training for developing middle-level workforce in the emerging business, to develop entrepreneurship and to serve as a link to mainstream higher education.

The principles that should guide a community college are:

- To offer programmes and courses of instruction up to the *Associate Degree* Level comprising career-oriented technical education, courses facilitating credit transfer to a three-year undergraduate degree programme and courses for workforce development and continuing education.
- To serve as a link between secondary school education and mainstream undergraduate education.
- To adopt a broad range of instructional methods and techniques to accommodate students of varied backgrounds, abilities and interests.
- To take a leadership role in shaping the direction of the communities by Enriching and enhancing the partnerships between the communities which they serve and the community colleges.
- To serve as an institutional support system for life-long learning.

2.1 ***Statement of Values:*** The set of values that shall guide the establishment and Operation of a community college include the following:

- The curriculum and programmes of a community college shall conform to the minimum standards set by an authority to be established for this purpose.
- Community college shall avoid unnecessary duplication of programmes by cooperating and coordinating with other similar agencies in the area.
- Community colleges shall maintain innovative learning environments to encourage creativity and the acquisition of knowledge and skills that prepare students for changing work environments, responsible citizenship, and leading rewarding lives.
- Community Colleges shall strive to serve the community by providing facilities for cultural enrichment, promoting economic development and partnerships, and by providing leadership and college talent to meet community needs. Keeping these in mind, the programmes offered by a community college should include:

A. *Occupational Education:* Programmes / courses designed to meet the increasing demand for technicians, semi-professional workers and skilled crafts-persons for employment by the industry, business and government as also those with entrepreneurial skills to establish and run small industries / businesses.

B. *College Transfer Education:* Courses in arts and science and pre-professional programmes of equal grade and quality as those provided in undergraduate colleges to facilitate transfer of credits to an undergraduate degree programme.

C. *General Education:* Courses that address the knowledge and skills required and expected of all educated persons. The elements that embody the essence of general education are:

- Language and Communication skills
- Interpersonal and human relations skills
- Basic IT skills
- Critical thinking and life-long learning skills
- Understanding culture and society

D. *Continuing Education:* The courses in this category address the needs of the adults in the region to acquire new skills and /or up date their skills and enable them to continue their learning experiences.

2.2 Eligibility of Students

A. The programmes of the community college shall be designed to serve all youth and adults who can benefit from one of its programmes / courses in accordance with its basic philosophy of universal access to higher education.

B. There shall be no upper age limit for admission to the community college. Persons eligible for general admission to the community college are high school graduates, or the equivalent, or those who are at least eighteen years of age, and are able to benefit from a programme at the community college. Other persons may apply to the admissions committee of the community college for special consideration for admittance of the community college.

C. *Admission to Specific Programs:* Applicants also may be required to meet other reasonable criteria for admission to any program or course within the community college to ensure that they possess the potential to meet program requirements. *A person applying to enter the Associate Degree programme shall be a higher secondary school graduate or should have passed an equivalent examination* (A pass in the 12th Standard of equivalent).

D. *Full-time and Part-time Students:* Persons are eligible to participate in the community college programs on either a full-time or part-time basis.

2.3 Length of Term

A. *Semester System:* The community colleges shall operate on a semester system on a year round schedule. The normal pattern is an odd semester (July - November) and even semester (December to April)

B. *Short-term Programmes:* Special programs on a short-term basis may be offered any time of the year.

C. *Day and Evening Programmes:* Instruction for students shall be offered in the community colleges in day and evening programs.

D. *Availability of Facilities:* Normally, the facilities will be in use for full day and evening programs of the community colleges for six days per week (Monday through Saturday). Insofar as possible and practicable, the facilities may me made available for community use.

3. Programme

The community colleges shall be institutions admitting a highly heterogeneous group of students in terms of levels of education, age, knowledge, skills, etc. The heterogeneity of the entrants could also be in terms of what they expect from the community college. It is possible to visualize five distinct categories of people who may seek admission to programmes of ICCS:

- Drop-outs from formal system of education but looking for a breakthrough to acquire skills in order to earn their livelihood.

- Those interested in acquiring skills in a particular trade which they wish to pursue.
- Employed people interested in updating their skills
- Displaced workers who need to acquire new skills to find jobs in the emerging job market; It is likely that the entrants belonging to this category will be middle-aged people (people in their 40s).
- Those who could not enter mainstream higher education and seek to do so via community colleges.

Community College shall build into their programmes a high degree of flexibility to ensure that community colleges are relevant and can be meaningful players in the higher education system. All community colleges shall offer the following programmes:

- A two-year credit-based *Associate Degree programme* for high-school graduates on completion of which those who desire should be permitted to enter mainstream higher education via later entry to the *final year / second year of the undergraduate programmes*
- A one year credit-based *Diploma* (in a certain trade) for those who can spend only one year with a provision that will allow them to enter the 2nd year of the Associate programme.
- Shorter duration non-credit courses leading to award of *Certificates*;
- Customized on-site or off-site short-term training programmes for personnel of a particular industry or a group of industries.

In the actual running of these programmes it is not necessary to offer each one of them as a separate programme. It is perfectly feasible to design the Associate Degree programme to subsume within it the Diploma and certificate programmes.

3.1 *Structure and Content:* the two-year Associate Degree program has to be harmonized with the 3-year bechelor's degree programmes. As mentioned earlier the contents shall have components related to:

- Occupational Education
- College Transfer Education
- General Education

The first year of the programme should focus on occupational education and general educations so that students who desire to take up a job on successful completion of the first year of the programme will receive a Diploma in the concerned vocation / trade they have chosen. The second year of the programme shall have courses related to college transfer education acceptable as equivalent to the *first year / first two years* of an undergraduate degree programme.

Appropriate courses in each of these three broad components have be designed and built into the programme. *A general idea of the distribution of credits that could be considered is given below:*

First Year of the Associate Degree Programme / Diploma Programme

Content	No. of Credits	No. of Hours
Language Skills	4	64
Communication and Inter-Personal Relation Skills	4	64
IT Skills	4	64
Entrepreneurial Skills	3	48
Vocation / Occupation (including practicum) (4 Courses)	12	192
Internship* (6 weeks of Internship @ 9 hours per day in real-life environment through understanding with user industries)	9	432
Total 36 Credits		864 hours

Content	No. of Credits	No. of Hours
English	3	48
Second Language	3	48
Environment Studies	3	48
Six Courses relevant to College Transfers (Area to be chosen by the candidates)	18	288
Internship* (6 weeks of Internship @ 9 hours per day in real-life environment through understanding with user industries)	9	432
Total 36 Credits		864 hours

**The effectiveness of the community college system will depend to a large extent on the involvement and participation of potential uses industries. In fact these should serve as practice schools and training in these real life environments will be the* *hallmark of ICCS that will set it apart from the existing system of vocational training.*

3.2 Designing the Curriculum and Industrial Partnerships

Effective and meaningful partnerships with industries and other organisations will be the backbone for a sustainable ICCS. Community College in a region should necessarily have MOUs with industries in the region. This partnership will help the ICCS in several ways. Active involvement and participation of potential user organisations is essential in terms of:

- Inputs in the design of courses / curriculum
- Inputs as members in various bodies of the ICCS such as advisory board, boards of studies, etc.
- Expert manpower to serve as part-time instructors
- Supervisors / Counsellors in on –the –job training in real life situations / locations (Internship)
- Placement of products of ICCS

4. *Accreditation and Governance*

A crucial factor for the success of the proposed community college system would be the establishment of an agency that will:

- Oversee the operation and development of community colleges in the country
- Function as an agency to establish benchmarks and standards to monitor and control quality
- Formulate and implement appropriate and relevant policy guidelines

In order to ensure the creation and proper functioning of a system of community colleges in the country it is imperative that a statutory body is established. This body (referred to hereinafter as ICCS) shall be the sole authority on the community college system in India.

(a) The ICCS shall evolve policies and standards for the establishment, development and administration of

community colleges and ensure their implementation.

(b) The ICCS shall have the authority to control and expend funds appropriated by law, and to accept from any government or governmental department or agency or any public or private body or from any other source, grants or contributions or money or property which may be used for or in aid of any of its purposes.

(c) The responsibility for initiating a request for the establishment of a community college shall rest with the state / local government / private bodies functioning in the political subdivision(s) to be served by the proposed community college. Before a community college can be approved by the ICCS, a survey under the supervision of the ICCS shall be conducted to determine:

- *Need for a community college:* The region to be served by a community college shall show evidence of the need for a community college and a continuing opportunity for placement of a sufficient number of graduates in employment and in colleges and universities to justify the programmes.
- *Evidence of Interest on the Part of Employers:* For the programme of occupational / technical education to be successful in the long run, employers in the region to be served by the community college should show an active interest in the development of curricula which reflect local needs and show a capacity to employ graduates. Active participation on the part of local leaders is important in gaining acceptance for employment of community college graduates, and in encouraging present employees in the region to use the community college to develop additional skills and to keep abreast of changes in technology affecting their jobs.
- *Evidence of Student Interest:* As a general standard, an area served by a community

colleges shall have 25000 or more students graduating from its secondary schools per year. Evidence shall indicate that from the number of current high school graduates and the number of interested adults in the area served, those who can be expected to attend the proposed community college shall be sufficient to assure a student body of at least 1000 full-time equivalent at the community college.

(d) The ICCS shall satisfy itself that the proposed community college has adequate infrastructure in terms of faculty, buildings and physical space, laboratory, library, etc and for future expansion.

(e) *Governing Board:* Every community college shall have a governing board consisting of:

- Principal of the community college
- Members appointed by the state government
- Representatives of local governments / municipal bodies in to be served by the college
- Representatives from industries in the area
- Representatives from Universities / colleges in the area
- Representatives of faculty of the community college
- Representative(s) from ICCS

4.1 *Accreditation:* the ICCS shall also function as the national agency to accredit community colleges in the country. The assessment shall be made with reference to a set a parameters so that the standing of a college can be compared with what is ideal and also with other similar institutions. The ICCS shall develop guidelines for accreditation involving the following criteria similar to those evolved by NAAC:

- Curricular Aspects
- Teaching, Learning and Evaluation
- Consultancy and Extension
- Infrastructure and Learning Resources
- Student Placement / Linkages with Business and Industry

- Management
- Healthy Practices

4.2 *Affiliation:* A principal objective of the community college system proposed here is to fill existing gaps and create a more meaningful system of post-higher secondary vocational education system in the country. A characteristic feature of the proposed system is the suggestion for establishing formal links between the proposed community colleges and the system of Higher Education being offered by the existing colleges and universities through lateral entry. This requires that a suitable mechanism for recognition and affiliation of the Associate Degree programmes for Community Colleges to facilitate lateral entry to undergraduate programmes in mainstream higher education institutions is established. This means that community colleges approved by the ICCS should seek affiliation for their Associate Degree programmes to universities in their geographical area. Universities, in turn, have to evolve and implement standards for granting affiliation to Community Colleges. Even at present most of our universities are of the *'affiliating'* type and have evolved suitable mechanisms for this purpose. This needs to be extended to include community colleges under ICCS. The following are important criteria in granting affiliation to a Community College:

- An area served by a Community College shall have 25000 or more students graduating per year from its secondary schools. Evidence shall indicate that there will at least be 500 full-time students at the Community College within three years of its establishment.
- Provisions of a suitable site: The agency proposing to set up a community college shall provide sufficient land, both for the initial establishment of the college and for future expansion, acceptable to the University; As a general standard the site shall consist of 2 acres

or more in an urban area that is easily accessible. Existing institutions meeting the requirements could be encouraged to house community colleges.

- The admission requirement and curriculum in the Community College especially for the Associate Degree programme shall conform to the criteria set by the University in terms of minimum eligibility requirements for admission, course contents, credit hours and evaluation methods.
- The affiliating university shall also evolve criteria for minimum standards for basic infrastructure for basic infrastructure required in terms of:
    - Adequate number of suitably qualified faculty
    - Classrooms
    - Laboratory
    - Formal linkages / MOUs with Industries / businesses in the region for practice school
    - Library

4.3 *Faculty:* The Community Colleges shall employ competent faculty members qualified to accomplish the mission and goals of the institution. When determining acceptable qualifications of its faculty, a community college shall give primary consideration to the highest earned degree in the discipline. For all cases, the institution is responsible fro justifying and documenting the qualifications of its faculty. A general guideline shall be that faculty that teach in the Associate Degree Programme must be eligible to teach in a 3-year college. However, lower qualifications for faculty teaching associate degree courses not designed for transfer to the undergraduate degree courses not designed for transfer to the undergraduate degree may be acceptable if they have demonstrated competencies in the discipline. The general guidelines for recruitment of faculty shall be as below:

- Faculty teaching credit courses at the Associate degree level transferable to an undergraduate degree programme shall have equivalent qualifications in the discipline applicable to members of faculty in a college / university.
- Faculty teaching associate degree courses not designed for transfer to the undergraduate degree shall have master's degree in the teaching discipline and competencies that are appropriate to support its teaching.

4.4 *Placement:* A Community College shall have a placement cell and establish links with the local industries, businesses and other potential employers of the products of the college.

5. *Models of Community Colleges:*

Several possible models are available for establishing community colleges. The most appropriate model (considering the prevailing circumstances and conditions in the area in which the community college has to be set up) has to be identified and adopted. The basic guideline shall be optimum utilization of available physical facilities / infrastructure in a geographical area. It is not very uncommon to find schools and colleges whose physical facilities are under-utilized. The four possible models for establishing community colleges are:

- Two-year branch campus of higher secondary schools
- Community College in an Industrial cluster
- Independent modern community college
- Upgrading of Polytechnics

Finance: ICCS shall evolve and adopt policies to ensure that community college education is accessible to those who may be hardest to reach but are in great need of the service of community colleges. ICCS shall encourage approved community college to offer the complete range of programmes identified and seek non-traditional revenue streams by creating their own set of courses. Community colleges will also design and offer programmes in collaboration with user industries to generate revenue.

A Schematic Representation

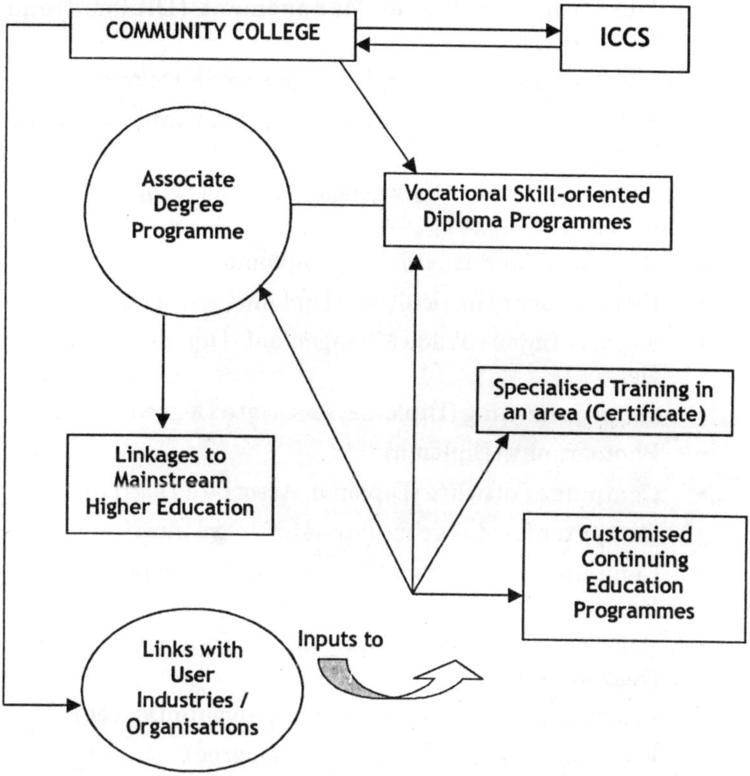

Appendix

Sample List of Trades / Vocations (Illustrative, not exhaustive)

Occupational:

- Two- Wheeler Mechanism (Diploma, Associate Degree)
- Four Wheeler mechanism (Diploma, Associate Degree)
- Fashion Design (Diploma, Associate Degree)
- Pottery (Diploma)
- Office Management and Secretarial practice (Diploma, Associate Degree)
- Web Designing (Diploma)
- Desktop Publishing (certificate, Diploma)

- Air-Conditioning and Refrigeration (Diploma and Associate Degree)
- Ticketing and Travel Management (Diploma and Associate Degree)
- Hotel Management (Diploma, Associate Degree)
- Bakery and Confectionary (Diploma and Associate Degree)
- Footwear and Leather goods manufacturing (Diploma, Associate Degree)
- Beautician and Health care (Diploma)
- Floriculture / Horticulture (Diploma, Associate Degree)
- Export / Import Trade Management (Diploma, Associate Degree)
- Organic farming (Diploma, Associate Degree)
- Photography (Diploma)
- Computer Software (Diploma, Associate Degree)
- Computer hardware maintenance (Diploma)
- Computerised Financial Accounting (Diploma, Associate Degree)
- Sales and Marketing Management (Diploma, Associate Degree)
- Printing Technology (Diploma, Associate Degree)
- Electronics (Diploma, Associate Degree)
- Small Home Appliances Service and Repair (Diploma)
- Multipurpose Rural Development worker (Diploma)
- Multipurpose Health Worker (Diploma)
- Agro-farming (Diploma, Associate Degree)

20
Publications

20.1 Books

1. Alphonse, Xavier, *"Changing Track"* – Community Colleges in India, AIACHE Publications, New Delhi. – *December 1996.*
2. Alphonse, Xavier, *"An Introduction to the Community College System (Tamil)*, MS University Publications, Tirunelveli, *September, 1998.*
3. Alphonse, Xavier, *"Including the Excluded": History of the Community Colleges in India*, MCRDCE Publications, Chennai, *January, 1999.*
4. Alphonse, Xavier, Editor, *"People Building Business" : Proceedings of the National Workshop on Community College System*, MCRDCE Publications, Chennai *February, 2000.*
5. Alphonse, Xavier, *Reaching Out:* History of the Community College movement an Update, MCRDCE Publications, Chennai, *July 2001.*
6. Alphonse, Xavier, *Mismatch: Establishing and Developing Community Colleges in India*, MCRDCE Publication, Chennai, *June 2002.*
7. Alphonse, Xavier, *We Shall Overcome : A Textbook on Life Coping Skills*, MCRDCE Publication, Chennai, *March 2004.*
8. Alphonse, Xavier, *Best to the Least – Profile of 80 Community Colleges in India*, MCRDCE Publication, Chennai, *November 2004.*

9. Alphonse, Xavier, *Walking the Extra Mile: A Textbook on Interpersonal Relationship and Communication Skills*, MCRDCE Publication, Chennai, *March 2005.*
10. Alphonse, Xavier, *Computer Made Easy: A Textbook on Basic Computing Skills*, MCRDCE Publication, Chennai, *March 2005.*
11. Alphonse, Xavier, *Miracles of Hope – Success Stories of the Community College Students*, MCRDCE Publication, Chennai, *March 2005.*
12. Alphonse, Xavier, and Xavier, Peter, *Neglected Majority - Problem of School Dropouts and Possible Alternatives*, MCRDCE Publication, Chennai, *March 2005.*
13. Alphonse, Xavier, *Marching with the Marginalised – The Contribution of MCRDCE to the Community College Movement in India (1995-2005)*, MCRDCE Publication, Chennai, *December 2005.*
14. Alphonse, Xavier, *Community College Empowerment Endorsed – The History of Recognition and Accreditation of Community Colleges (1995-2005).* MCRDCE Publication, Chennai, *December 2005.*
15. Alphonse, Xavier, *Bloom and Blossom : A source book on eco-friendly sustainable agriculture for integrated rural development*, co-authored by Mr. S.A.Kader Ibrahim MCRDCE Publication, Chennai, *December 2005.*

20.2 Newsletters

1. MCRDCE Newsletter, No. 1, *January 2001.*
2. MCRDCE Newsletter, No. 2, *September 2002.*
3. MCRDCE Newsletter, No. 3, *March 2004.*
4. MCRDCE Newsletter, No. 4, *October 2004.*
5. MCRDCE Newsletter, No. 5, *October 2005.*

20.3 Articles

I. National

(i) New Frontiers in Education

1. Alphonse, Xavier, *"To Include the Excluded", New Frontiers in Education, AIACHE*, New Delhi, *Vol. 27:4, October – December 1997.*

2. Alphonse, Xavier, *"Community Colleges : A Policy Report"*, *New Frontiers in Education*, AIACHE, New Delhi, *Vol. 24:2, April – June 1999.*
3. Alphonse, Xavier, *"Community Colleges: Norms and Guidelines for Recognition and Approval" New Frontiers in Education*, AIACHE, New Delhi, *Vol. 24:4, October – December 1999.*
4. Alphonse, Xavier, *"Community College System towards Vertical Mobility" New Frontiers in Education*, AIACHE, New Delhi, *Vol. 30:3, July-September 2000.*
5. Alphonse, Xavier, *"The Stages and Dynamics of the Community College Movement in India (1995 – 2001)"*, *New Frontiers in Education*, AIACHE, New Delhi, *Vol. 31 No. 2 April – June, 2001.*
6. Alphonse, Xavier, *"Best to the Least: Community College Movement in India- An Update" New Frontiers in Education*, AIACHE, New Delhi, *Vol. 32:2, April-June 2002.*
7. Alphonse, Xavier, *"Beyond the Frontiers : The Growth and Future of the Community College Movement in India (1995-2004)"*, *New Frontiers in Education*, AIACHE, New Delhi, *Vol. 34:2 April-June 2004.*
8. Alphonse, Xavier, *"Marching with the Marginalised : The Community College Movement in Fulfillment of its Mission"*, *New Frontiers in Education*, AIACHE, New Delhi, *Vol. 34:4 October – December 2004.*
9. *Alphonse, Xavier,* "Community Colleges – *Enlightenment and Empowerment," New Frontiers in Education*, AIACHE, New Delhi, *Vol. 35:3, July – September 2005.*
10. *Document – "Indian Community College System' New Frontiers in Education*, AIACHE, New Delhi, *Vol. 35:3, July – September 2005.*

(ii) University News

1. Alphonse, Xavier, *"Madras Community College – An Educational Alternative"*, *University News*, New Delhi, *Vol. 34:36, 2nd of September 1996.*

2. Alphonse, Xavier & Pushparaj, *"Madurai Community College – An Educational Alternative"*, *University News*, New Delhi, *Vol. 35:41, 13th of October 1997.*
3. Alphonse, Xavier & Joe Rajan, *"Melrosapuram Rural Community College – An Educational Alternative"*, *University News*, New Delhi, *Vol. 36:28, 8th of June, 1998.*
4. *"Community College Movement"*, *University News*, New Delhi, *Vol. 37:1, 4th of January 1999.*
5. Alphonse, Xavier, *"Community College: Meeting Society's Needs"*, *University News*, New Delhi, *Vol. 37:36, 6th of September 1999.*
6. *"Striving for Recognition – Community College"*, *University News*, New Delhi, *Vol. 37:44, 1st of November 1999.*
7. *Alphonse, Xavier*, "Seminar on Community Colleges", University News, *New Delhi*, Vol. 38:17, 24th of April 2000.
8. Alphonse, Xavier, *"Community College Movement": An Overview*, *University News*, New Delhi, *Vol. 38:35, 28th of August 2000.*
9. Alphonse, Xavier, *"Community Colleges: A National Phenomenon"*, *University News*, New Delhi, *Vol. 39:26, June 25 – July 1, 2001.*
10. Xavier Alphonse and James C., *"Best to the Least : Education for Livelihood – Community Colleges in India", University News, Vol.42 No. 14, April 5-11, 2004.*
11. Alphonse, Xavier, *"Seminar on Indian Community College System", Campus News, University News*, New Delhi, *Vol. 43:10, March 7-13, 2005.*
12. Alphonse, Xavier, *"National Consultation of Community Colleges in India", Campus News, University News*, New Delhi, *Vol. 43:16, April 18-24, 2005.*
13. Alphonse, Xavier, *"Empowerment of Socio-economically Weaker Sections through the Community College System and the Support of the Universities in India", University News, New Delhi, Vol.43:47, November 21-27, 2005.*

(iii) Other Publications

1. *Community Colleges: Experiments and Challenges, AIACHE Newsletter*, New Delhi, *April, 1999.*
2. Alphonse, Xavier, *"Community College System towards Vertical Mobility" National Qualification Framework, 25th and 26th of July 2000.*
3. Alphonse, Xavier, *"Community College Movement in India – From Adoption to Extension Nationwide, Changing Colleges, December 2000.*
4. Alphonse, Xavier, *"Ten Years of Community Colleges in India", The New Leader, October 16-31, 2005.*

(iv) Newspaper Articles

1. Alphonse, Xavier, *"To Include the Excluded," The Hindu*, Chennai, *20th January 1998* and *27th January 1998.*
2. Alphonse, Xavier, *"Empowering the Disadvantaged", The Hindu, 9th of May 2000.*
3. *"Community College System on Rise", Madras Universitas*, Vol. 27 No. 2, *1st of September 2003.*
4. *"Education for a Livelihood", The Hindu, 21st of December 2005.*
5. Alphonse, Xavier, *"Learning for Livelihood", Frontline*, Vol. 23 No. 2, *January 28-February 10, 2006.*

(v) Jivan

1. Alphonse, Xavier, *"Community Education Centre Inaugurated in Chennai", Jivan, April 1999.*
2. Alphonse, Xavier, *"Experiments and Challenges", Jivan, April 1999.*
3. Alphonse, Xavier, *"National Workshop on Community Colleges", Jivan, August 2000.*
4. Alphonse, Xavier, *"Best to the Least", Jivan, January 2003.*

II. International

1. *"A New Breed of College comes to India", The Community College Times, 29th of July 1997.*

2. *"South India Community Colleges Continue to grow", Community Colleges for International Development, August 2002.*
3. *"Community Colleges in India look to the West", Community College Times*, American Association of Community Colleges, *Vol: 15, No: 21, 28th of October 2003.*

20.4 Monographs

1. Alphonse, Xavier, *"Community College- A National Phenomenon": The Stages and Dynamics of the Community College Movement in India (1995-2001)*, MCRDCE Publications, Chennai, *March 2001.*
2. Alphonse, Xavier, *"The Contribution of MCRDCE to the Community College Movement in India (1995 - 2001)"*, MCRDCE Publication, Chennai, *December 2001.*
3. Alphonse, Xavier, *"The Growth and Future of Community College Movement in India (1995-2003)"*, published on the Occasion of *Sixth Consultation on Community Colleges in India*, MCRDCE Publications, Chennai, *July 2003.*

Bibliography

Books

1. Ramakrishnan, Ganapati, *"Community College for India"*, Madras Institute for Development Education, Chennai *– 1980.*
2. Alphonse, Xavier, *"Changing Track"* – Community Colleges in India, AIACHE Publications, New Delhi – *December 1996.*
3. Alphonse, Xavier, *"An Introduction to the Community College System (Tamil)*, MS University Publications, Tirunelveli – *September 1998.*
4. Alphonse, Xavier, *"Including the Excluded": History of the Community Colleges in India*, MCRDCE Publications, Chennai – *January 1999.*
5. Alphonse, Xavier, Editor, *"People Building Business": Proceedings of the National Workshop on Community College System, February 2000*, MCRDCE Publications, Chennai – *September 2000.*
6. Alphonse, Xavier, *"Reaching Out": Community College Movement in India – An Update*, MCRDCE Publications, Chennai, *July 2001.*
7. Alphonse, Xavier, *The Contribution of MCRDCE to the Community College Movement in India (1995 - 2001)*, MCRDCE Publication, Chennai, *December 2001.*
8. Alphonse, Xavier, *Mismatch: Establishing and Developing Community Colleges in India*, MCRDCE Publication, Chennai, *June 2002.*

9. Alphonse, Xavier, *The Growth and Future of the Community College Movement in India (1995 - 2003)*, MCRDCE Publication, Chennai, *July 2003*.
10. Alphonse, Xavier, *"We Shall Overcome": A textbook on Life Coping Skills*, MCRDCE Publication, Chennai, *March 2004*.
11. Alphonse, Xavier, *"Best to the Least – Profile of Community Colleges in India"*, MCRDCE Publication, Chennai, *November 2004*.
12. Alphonse, Xavier, *Walking the Extra Mile: A Textbook on Interpersonal Relationship and Communication Skills*, MCRDCE Publication, Chennai, *March 2005*.
13. Alphonse, Xavier, *Computer Made Easy: A Textbook on Basic Computing Skills*, MCRDCE Publication, Chennai, *March 2005*.
14. Alphonse, Xavier, *Miracles of Hope – Success Stories of the Community College Students*, MCRDCE Publication, Chennai, *March 2005*.
15. *Neglected Majority* - The Problem of School Dropouts and Possible Alternatives, Co-authored by Dr. Peter Xavier, S.J., MCRDCE Publication, Chennai, *March 2005*.
16. Alphonse, Xavier, *Marching with the Marginalised : The Contribution of MCRDCE to the Community College Movement in India*, MCRDCE Publication, Chennai, *December 2005*.
17. Alphonse, Xavier, *Community College Empowerment Endorsed : The History of Recognition and Accreditation of Community Colleges in India*, MCRDCE Publication, Chennai, *December 2005*.
18. Alphonse, Xavier, *Bloom and Blossom : A source book on eco-friendly sustainable agriculture for integrated rural development*, co-authored by Mr. S.A.Kader Ibrahim MCRDCE Publication, Chennai, *December 2005*.

Articles

1. *S.N.Mehrotra*, "The College and the Community", *New Frontiers in Education*, AIACHE, New Delhi, *Vol. 2:2, 1971*.
2. *D'Scuza, S. Victor*, "Restructuring Higher Education in India – Relevance of the American Community College",

New Frontiers in Education, AIACHE, New Delhi, *Vol. 21:4, 1991.*

3. *Rao, Sudha K.*, "Community Colleges in India: Need and Relevance", *New Frontiers in Education*, AIACHE, New Delhi, *Vol. 24:3, 1994.*
4. *Alphonse, Xavier*, "Madras Community College – An Educational Alternative", *University News*, New Delhi, *Vol. 34:36, September 2, 1996.*
5. *Heimer, Muriel Kay*, "The Community College : Opportunity, Accessibility, Excellence, *New Frontiers in Education, Vol. 27:1, 1997.*
6. "A New Breed of College comes to India", The Community College Times, *July 29, 1997.*
7. *Alphonse, Xavier & Pushparaj*, "Madurai Community College – An Educational Alternative", *University News*, New Delhi, *Vol. 35:41, October 13, 1997.*
8. *Alphonse, Xavier*, "To Include the Excluded", *New Frontiers in Education*, AIACHE, New Delhi, *Vol. 27:4, October – December 1997.*
9. *Alphonse, Xavier*, "To Include the Excluded", *The Hindu*, Madras, *January 20, 1998 and January 27, 1998.*
10. *Alphonse, Xavier & Joe Rajan*, "Melrosapuram Rural Community College – An Educational Alternative", *University News*, New Delhi, *Vol. 36 : 23, June 8, 1998.*
11. "Community College Movement", *University News*, New Delhi, *Vol. 37:1, January 1999.*
12. Community Colleges: Experiments and Challenges", *AIACHE Newsletter*, New Delhi, *April, 1999.*
13. *Alphonse, Xavier*, "Community Colleges : A Policy Report", *New Frontiers in Education*, AIACHE, New Delhi, *Vol. 29:2, April – June 1999.*
14. *Alphonse, Xavier*, Community College: Meeting Society's Needs", *University News*, New Delhi, *Vol. 37:36, September 6, 1999.*
15. *Alphonse, Xavier*, "Community Colleges: Norms and Guidelines for Recognition and Approval" *New Frontiers in Education, Vol. 29:4, October – December 1999.*
16. "Striving for Recognition – Community College", *University News*, New Delhi, *Vol. 37:44, November 1, 1999. (Campus News).*

17. Bhattacharya, Sandhya, "Community College Initiative", *Education World*, April 2000.

18. *Alphonse, Xavier*, "Seminar on Community Colleges", *University News*, New Delhi, *Vol. 38:17, April 24, 2000. (Campus News).*

19. *Alphonse, Xavier*, "Empowering the Disadvantaged", *The Hindu, May 9, 2000.*

20. *Alphonse, Xavier*, "Community College System towards Vertical Mobility" *National Qualification Framework, 25th and 26th of July 2000.*

21. *Alphonse, Xavier*, "Community College Movement": An Overview, *University News*, New Delhi, *Vol. 38:35, August 28, 2000.*

22. *Alphonse, Xavier*, "Community College System towards Vertical Mobility" *New Frontiers in Education, Vol. 30:3 July-September 2000.*

23. *Alphonse, Xavier*, "Community College Movement in India – From Adoption to Extension Nationwide, Changing Colleges, *December 2000.*

24. *Alphonse, Xavier*, "The Stages and Dynamics of the Community College Movement in India (1995 – 2001), New Frontiers in Education, AIACHE, New Delhi, *Vol. 31 No. 2 April – June, 2001.*

25. *Alphonse, Xavier*, "Community Colleges: A National Phenomenon", *University News, June 25 – July 1, 2001.*

26. *Alphonse, Xavier*, "Best to the Least: Community College Movement in India- An Update" *New Frontiers in Education, Vol. 32:2 April-June 2002.*

27. *"Community College System on Rise"*, Madras Universitas, Vol. 27 No.2, *September 1, 2003.*

28. *Alphonse, Xavier*, "The Growth and Future of the Community College Movement in India (1995-2003)", *July 2003.*

29. *"Community Colleges in India look to the West"*, Community College Times, American Association of Community Colleges, *Vol:15 No: 21, 28th of October 2003.*

30. *Xavier Alphonse and James C.*, "Best to the Least : Education for Livelihood – Community Colleges in India", *University News, Vol.42 No. 14, April 5-11, 2004.*

31. *Alphonse, Xavier*, "Beyond the Frontiers : The Growth and Future of the Community College Movement in India (1995-2004)", *New Frontiers in Education, Vol. 34:2 April-June 2004.*

32. "Access and Equity in Higher Education", Selections from University News – 15, Association of Indian Universities, New Delhi, *2004.* Alphonse, Xavier, "Community College: Meeting Society's Needs"', *University News*, Vol. 37 No. 36, September 6, 1999, p.131-144.

33. *Alphonse, Xavier*, "Marching with the Marginalised : The Community College Movement in Fulfillment of its Mission", *New Frontiers in Education*, AIACHE, New Delhi, *Vol. 34:4 October – December 2004.*

34. *Alphonse, Xavier*, "Seminar on Indian Community College System", *University News*, New Delhi, *Vol. 43:10, March 7-13, 2005.*

35. *Alphonse, Xavier*, "National Consultation of Community Colleges in India", *Campus News, University News*, New Delhi, *Vol. 43:16, April 18-24, 2005.*

36. *Alphonse, Xavier*, "Community Colleges – Enlightenment and Empowerment," *New Frontiers in Education, AIACHE, New Delhi, Vol. 35:3, July – September 2005.*

37. *Document* – "Indian Community College System" *New Frontiers in Education, AIACHE, New Delhi, Vol. 35:3, July – September 2005.*

38. *Alphonse, Xavier*, "Empowerment of Socio-economically Weaker Sections through the Community College System and the Support of the Universities in India", *University News*, New Delhi, *Vol.43 No.47, November 21-27, 2005.*

39. *Alphonse, Xavier*, "Learning for Livelihood", *Frontline, Vol.23 No.2, January 28-February 10, 2006.*

Book Reviews

1. *Alphonse, Xavier*, "Changing Track": Plea for an Educational Alternative, *University News*, New Delhi, *Vol. 35:33, August 18, 1997.*

2. *Alphonse, Xavier*, "Changing Track" – Community Colleges in India, *The Hindu, September 9, 1997.*

3. *Alphonse, Xavier*, "Including the Excluded", *University News*, New Delhi, *Vol. 38:20, May 15, 2000.*
4. *Alphonse, Xavier*, "Including the Excluded", *The Hindu, August 8, 2000.*
5. *Alphonse, Xavier*, "Mismatch", *Southern Economist, Bangalore, October 1, 2003.*
6. *Alphonse, Xavier*, "Best to the Least: Profile of Community Colleges in India, *University News*, New Delhi, *Vol.43 No.47, November 21-27, 2005.*

News Paper Clippings

1. *"Education has to be responsive to Industry"*, The Hindu, August 19, 1992.
2. *"Needed : Community Colleges"*, The Hindu, 1994.
3. *"UGC to promote Community College"*, The Hindu, April 4, 1995.
4. *"Colleges asked to provide Work-Oriented Skills"*, The Hindu, July 2, 1996.
5. *"Education must be tuned to Societal Needs"*, The New Indian Express, August 5, 1996.
6. *"Community College Set Up"*, The Hindu, August 5, 1996.
7. *"Varsity Plans to start Community College"*, The Hindu, March 18, 1997.
8. *"Need to set up Community Colleges"*, The Hindu, April 16, 1997.
9. *"Community Colleges can Bridge Education, Employment Gap"*, The Indian Express, August 12, 1997.
10. *"Community College catering to the Society" – Pondicherry Panorama : A Feature*, The Hindu, May 30, 1998.
11. *"Community Colleges meet opens today"*, The Hindu, January 8, 1999.
12. *"Community Concept Hailed"*, The Hindu, January 12, 1999.
13. *"Corporation, Industry come together to generate Employment for school children"*, The New Indian Express, January 25, 1999.
14. *"Job Skills for the Underprivileged"* The Hindu, February 1, 1999.

15. *"Community Colleges : A Boon to Non-Formal Students"* The Hindu, May 29, 1999.

16. *"Making their dreams a reality"*, The Hindu, June 28, 1999.

17. *"Need for Alternative System of Education felt"*, News Today, February 19, 2000.

18. *Sankarnarayanan, Harini, "Affordable Higher Education for all – Community Colleges are fast becoming an Attractive Option, Reports"* The Economic Times, February 27, 2000.

19. *"Community College concept catching up in State"*, The Hindu, March 23, 2000.

20. *Alphonse, Xavier, "Empowering the Disadvantaged"* The Hindu, May 9, 2000. (Open Page, Education).

21. *"Bridge Gap between Education, Employment"*, New Today, May 21, 2000.

22. *"Meet on Community Colleges"*, The Times of India, Mumbai, September 21, 2000.

23. *"Accent on role of Community Colleges"*, The New Indian Express, October 10, 2000.

24. *"Separate authority for Community Colleges Mooted"*, News Today, October 11, 2000.

25. *"Call to promote Life-Oriented Education"*, The Hindu, October 13, 2000.

26. *"Building Youth for the Future"*, Nagaland Page, October 26, 2000.

27. *"Workshop on Community College"*, Nagaland Post, October 26, 2000.

28. *"Workshop on Community Colleges Inaugurated"* The New Indian Express, Kochi, 19th January, 2001.

29. *"Community Colleges : Centre looking for lead from TN"*, News Today, 19th February, 2001.

30. *"Alternative Colleges, an Emerging Concept"*, News Today, 23rd February 2001.

31. *"Community College workshop tan a ni"*, Hnethu, 15th of March 2001.

32. *"Community College seeks inclusion in 10th Plan"*, News Today, 5th of April 2001.

33. *"Recognition of Community Colleges urged"*, Trinity Mirror, 12th April 2001.

34. *"Community Educational System should recognised : MCRDCE"*, The Indian Express", 13th of April 2001.

35. *"Government assures Community Colleges of all help"*, News Today, 22nd of April 2001.

36. *"Community Colleges lauded"*, 2nd of August 2002.

37. *"Students make a beeline to Agri Community College – The Institution, first in Tamil Nadu to offer Job-Oriented Courses at nominal fees"*, The New Indian Express, 21st of April 2002.

38. *"Fostering Education"*, The Hindu, 29th of July 2002.

39. *"Community College comes up at YWCA"*, News Today, 2nd of August 2002.

40. *"Need to change education system stressed"*, News Today, 21st of August 2002.

41. *"St. Anne's to tie up with Delhi School"*, The New Indian Express, 1st of September 2002.

42. *"Education that ensures gainful employment"*, The Hindu, 5th of October 2002.

43. *"Community College system aiming at uplifting the marginalized"*, The New Indian Express, Kochi, 12th of October 2002.

44. *"Workshop on skill based education today"* The Times of India, Lucknow, 25th of October 2002.

45. *"Community Colleges start scripting course to success"*, The New Indian Express, 26th of December 2002.

46. *"Community College for poor students"*, The Hindu, Eluru, 26th of January 2003.

47. *"Community Colleges could help tackle dropout"*, Herald, 28th of April 2003.

48. *"Academics advocate Community College for Goa"*, Herald, 28th of April 2003.

49. *"Make me Fit for Life"*, The Herald, May 2-8, 2003.

50. *"Community Colleges ideal for dropouts"*, The Hindu, 31st of March 2004.

51. *"St. Aloysius College holds workshop on Community College"*, The Hitavada, 4th April 2004.

52. *"Interview / on Community Colleges"*, Mylapore Times, May 29 – June 4, 2004.

53. *"Fit for Life"*, The New Indian Express, City Express, 16th of June 2004.

54. *"We Shall Overcome"* – Book Review, The Hindu, 22nd June 2004.

55. *"NGO to start Community College"*, The New Indian Express, Trichy, 22nd of July 2004.

56. *"Community College launched"*, Bhopal Today, Chronicle, 31st of July 2004.

57. *"Panel formed to prepare comprehensive policy document"*, The Hindu, 10th of October 2004.

58. *"V-C pushes for 'para-formal' education"*, The Hindu, 13th of November 2004.

59. *"Book on Community Colleges released"*, Indian Express, 13th of November 2004.

60. *"VC outlines the key to higher education"*, News Today, 13th of November 2004.

61. *"HRD Ministry seeks report from UGC"*, The New Indian Express, 9th of February 2005.

62. *"Will Community College concept do the trick?"* News Today, 9th of February 2005.

63. *"Economic Growth linked to Community Colleges"*, City Express, 10th of February 2005.

64. *Integrate Community Colleges into Higher Education Scheme"*, The Hindu, 10th of February 2005.

65. *"Higher Education for all"*, The Hindu, Education Plus, 14th of February 2005.

66. *"Decision on 'potential for excellence status" to varsities by month-end"*, The Hindu, 7th of March 2005.

67. *"Thrust on Community Colleges for better education"*, Indian Express, 12th of March 2005.

68. *"Community Colleges need Government support"*, The Hindu, 12th of March 2005.

69. *"Community Colleges may be the answer"*, News Today, 13th of March 2005.

70. *"In service of poor"*, The Hindu, 15th of April 2005.

71. *"Empowering the powerless"*, The Hindu, 18th of April 2005.

72. *"Educate and Enlighten"*, Deccan Herald, 7th of July 2005.

73. *"Rural youths need help for empowerment"*, The New Indian Express, 3rd of August 2005.

74. *"Community Colleges play vital role"*, The Hindu, 12th of September 2005.

75. *"College to empower the poor"*, The Hindu, 9th of October 2005.

76. *"Community Colleges a boon to the poor"*, The New Indian Express, 7th of December 2005.

77. *"Empowering the Marginalised"*, Education Plus, The Hindu, 19th of December 2005.

78. *"Technical Courses for the tsunami victims"*, The Hindu, Vellore Edition, 20th of December 2005.

79. *"Education for a Livelihood"*, The Hindu, 21st of December 2005.

"Efforts of Community Colleges earn praise", *24th of December 2005.*

Index